Troodon
embryo

Megalosaurus
tooth

EYEWITNESS
DINOSAUR

Written by
DAVID LAMBERT

Kentrosaurus

DK

Ammonite
mould

Ammonite cast

Gila monster

Iguanodon hand

Ankylosaur scute
(bony plate)

Troodon

DK | Penguin Random House

Consultant Dr David Norman
Senior editor Rob Houston
Editorial assistant Jessamy Wood
Managing editors Julie Ferris, Jane Yorke
Managing art editor Owen Peyton Jones
Art director Martin Wilson
Associate publisher Andrew Macintyre
Picture researcher Louise Thomas
Production editor Melissa Latorre
Production controller Charlotte Oliver
Jacket designers Martin Wilson, Johanna Woolhead
Jacket editor Adam Powley

DK India
Editor Kingshuk Ghoshal
Designer Govind Mittal
DTP designers Dheeraj Arora, Preetam Singh
Project editor Suchismita Banerjee
Design manager Romi Chakraborty
Production manager Pankaj Sharma

Relaunch Edition (DK UK)
Editor Ashwin Khurana
Senior designers Rachael Grady, Spencer Holbrook
Managing editor Gareth Jones
Managing art editor Philip Letsu
Publisher Andrew Macintyre
Producer, pre-production Adam Stoneham
Senior producer Charlotte Cade
Jacket editor Maud Whatley
Jacket designer Laura Brim
Jacket design development manager Sophia MTT
Publishing director Jonathan Metcalf
Associate publishing director Liz Wheeler
Art director Phil Ormerod

Relaunch Edition (DK India)
Senior editor Neha Gupta
Art editor Deep Shikha Walia
Senior DTP designer Harish Aggarwal
DTP designers Anita Yadav, Pawan Kumar
Managing editor Alka Thakur Hazarika
Managing art editor Romi Chakraborty
CTS manager Balwant Singh
Jacket editorial manager Saloni Talwar
Jacket designers Govind Mittal, Suhita Dharamjit, Vidit Vashisht , Dhirendra Singh

This Eyewitness ® Guide has been conceived by
Dorling Kindersley Limited and Editions Gallimard

First published in Great Britain in 1990

This relaunch edition published in 2014
by Dorling Kindersley Limited,
80 Strand, London WC2R ORL

Copyright © 1990, 2002, 2007, 2014 Dorling Kindersley Limited, London
A Penguin Random House Company

19 4 6 8 10 9 7 5

025 – 196565 – July/14

A CIP catalogue record for this book is
available from the British Library.

ISBN 978-1-4093-4371-4

Printed in China

A WORLD OF IDEAS:
SEE ALL THERE IS TO KNOW

www.dk.com

Oviraptor egg

Contents

Ankylosaurus

Age of Dinosaurs

Dinosaurs ruled the Earth for 160 million years and ranged from huge creatures to animals no bigger than a hen. Dinosaurs ("terrible lizards") were reptiles, but instead of walking in a sprawling way like lizards, they walked upright, and some dinosaurs had feathers instead of scales. More than 1,000 species of dinosaur existed during the Age of Dinosaurs. Then 65 million years ago, they mysteriously died out, except for one group – the dinosaurs that we know as birds.

Opening in skull in front of eye reduced the weight of the skull

Neck with S-shaped curve

Hole between bones of lower jaw helped to lighten the skull

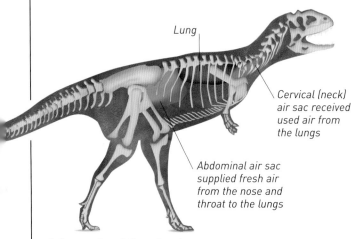

Lung

Cervical (neck) air sac received used air from the lungs

Abdominal air sac supplied fresh air from the nose and throat to the lungs

A breath of fresh air

Unlike modern reptiles, some dinosaurs, such as *Majungatholus*, had air sacs connected to their lungs, just as birds do. These sacs pushed a constant flow of fresh air through the lungs.

Fossil feathers

The brown fringes around the skeleton of this fossil *Microraptor* are traces of feathers. Some dinosaurs had downy feathers for warmth; others had showy feathers to attract a mate. *Microraptor*'s long feathers helped it to glide between trees.

Head of thigh bone points inwards to fit into the hip socket – this helps to keep the limb erect

Walking tall

The limb bones of dinosaurs show that they walked as mammals do, with their legs underneath the body. The limbs had to be strong as some dinosaur bodies weighed as much as a truck. Like many dinosaurs, *Tyrannosaurus* had high ankles and narrow feet. It walked on its toes, which helped it to move at speed.

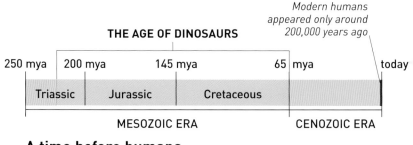

Modern humans appeared only around 200,000 years ago

THE AGE OF DINOSAURS

250 mya	200 mya	145 mya	65 mya	today
Triassic	Jurassic	Cretaceous		

MESOZOIC ERA   CENOZOIC ERA

A time before humans

Dinosaurs lived in the Mesozoic Era, about 250 to 65 million years ago (mya). This era is further divided into the Triassic, Jurassic, and Cretaceous periods. Other than birds, all dinosaurs died out long before the first humans appeared.

Reptile relations

During the Mesozoic Era, the seas were ruled by large non-dinosaur reptiles, such as the plesiosaurs, mosasaurs, and ichthyosaurs. *Elasmosaurus* was the longest-known plesiosaur, growing to lengths of up to 14 m (46 ft).

Extremely long neck
supported by 72 cervical
vertebrae (neck bones)

Flipper-shaped limb

Upright
hind limb

Green,
scaly
skin

Sprawling
leg

Thumblike digit
for grasping

Hand with three
main digits

Weight-bearing toe

Hingelike
ankle

Dinosaur features

Like all dinosaurs, *Monolophosaurus* stood upright thanks to its hip joints. It walked only on its hind limbs, using its heavy tail for balance. The dinosaur's third digits (fingers) could twist a little to face the other two digits, forming grasping hands.

Terrible lizards?

Evidence suggests that dinosaurs were warm-blooded and kept constant body temperatures. Modern reptiles, such as this basilisk lizard, are cold-blooded, which means they rely on the sun's heat for body warmth.

Different designs

Scientists divide dinosaurs into two groups according to how their hip bones are arranged. The saurischians included the plant-eating sauropods and the meat-eating theropods. The ornithischians were plant-eaters and included the ornithopods, as well as the plated, armoured, and horned dinosaurs. The family tree on pages 64–65 shows how all these dinosaurs were related.

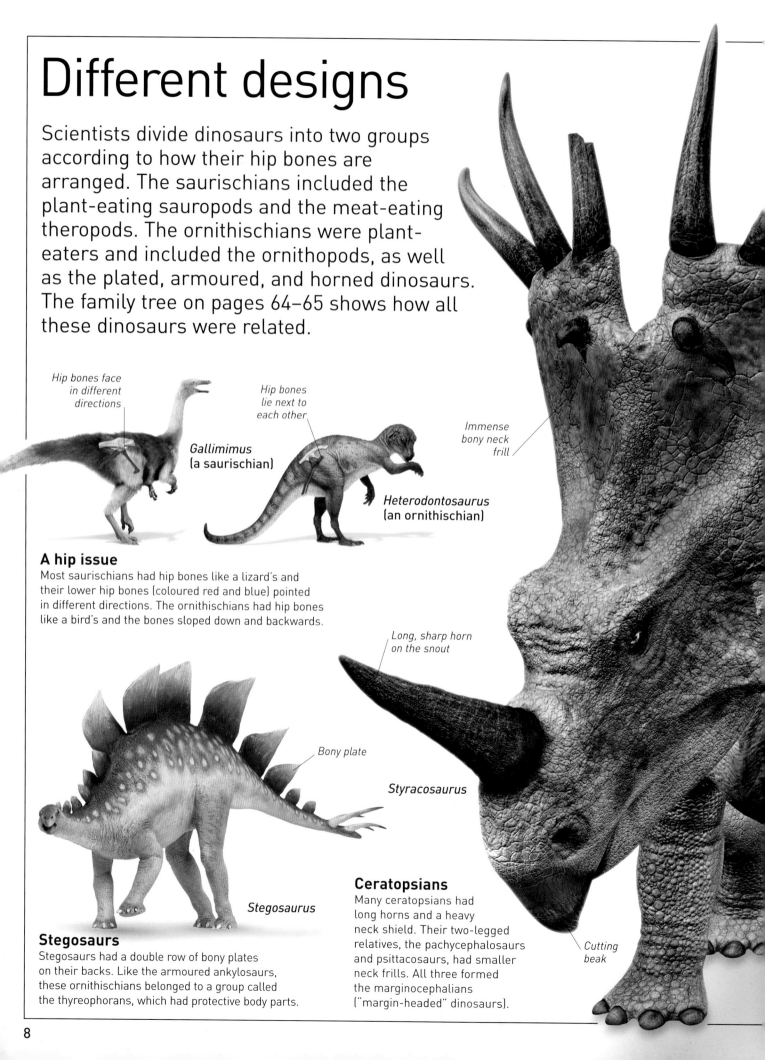

Hip bones face in different directions

Hip bones lie next to each other

Gallimimus
(a saurischian)

Heterodontosaurus
(an ornithischian)

Immense bony neck frill

A hip issue
Most saurischians had hip bones like a lizard's and their lower hip bones (coloured red and blue) pointed in different directions. The ornithischians had hip bones like a bird's and the bones sloped down and backwards.

Long, sharp horn on the snout

Bony plate

Styracosaurus

Stegosaurus

Ceratopsians
Many ceratopsians had long horns and a heavy neck shield. Their two-legged relatives, the pachycephalosaurs and psittacosaurs, had smaller neck frills. All three formed the marginocephalians ("margin-headed" dinosaurs).

Cutting beak

Stegosaurs
Stegosaurs had a double row of bony plates on their backs. Like the armoured ankylosaurs, these ornithischians belonged to a group called the thyreophorans, which had protective body parts.

Bony spike jutting from neck frill

Sauropods

These saurischians were the largest creatures ever to walk on Earth. Along with the prosauropods, the sauropods formed a group of long-necked plant-eaters called sauropodomorphs. These spread all over the world, and lived as far south as present-day Antarctica.

Immensely long neck

Long, whiplike tail

Ornithopods

Plant-eating ornithopods first appeared in the Jurassic Period. Early kinds were small and fast enough to outrun larger meat-eaters. Later ones included bulky *Muttaburrasaurus*, *Iguanodon*, and the hadrosaurs (duck-billed dinosaurs).

Bony bump on head

Sharp and horny beak

Heavy tail

Barosaurus

Muttaburrasaurus

Forelimb used as a foot

Pillarlike leg

Armoured bands

Bony tail club

Ankylosaurs

Ankylosaurs were a group of armoured ornithischians. Their four sturdy legs supported a barrel-shaped body. Some had a bony tail club, others sharp shoulder spikes.

Euoplocephalus

Ceratosaurus

Nose horn

Bladelike teeth

Theropods

Theropods were meat-eating saurischians. Most had sharp teeth, and clawed toes on strong, birdlike feet. They ranged from huge *Tyrannosaurus* to feathered animals no larger than a pigeon.

Triassic times

The Triassic Period lasted from around 250 to 200 million years ago. At this time, there was only a single continent surrounded by a mighty ocean. Deserts covered the land and flowering plants had yet to appear. Prehistoric reptiles and the reptilelike ancestors of mammals thrived in these conditions. Some reptiles, such as the pterosaurs, took to the air, while others swam in shallow seas. The first dinosaurs appeared in the second half of the Triassic Period.

The Triassic world
In this period, Earth's continents were joined together as a single landmass called Pangaea. Surrounding Pangaea was a single ocean, with a great inlet called the Tethys Sea.

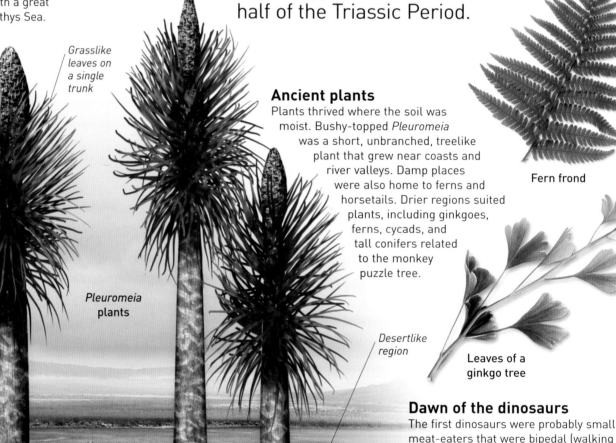

Grasslike leaves on a single trunk

Pleuromeia plants

Ancient plants
Plants thrived where the soil was moist. Bushy-topped *Pleuromeia* was a short, unbranched, treelike plant that grew near coasts and river valleys. Damp places were also home to ferns and horsetails. Drier regions suited plants, including ginkgoes, ferns, cycads, and tall conifers related to the monkey puzzle tree.

Fern frond

Desertlike region

Leaves of a ginkgo tree

Dawn of the dinosaurs
The first dinosaurs were probably small meat-eaters that were bipedal (walking on two legs). Plant-eaters, both bipedal and quadrupedal (walking on all fours), appeared at the end of the Triassic Period.

***Herrerasaurus* (228 mya)**
This bipedal hunter from Argentina is one of the earliest-known dinosaurs. Its long tail was used for balance when running.

Flexible neck

Reptiles take flight
Eudimorphodon was a flying reptile about 70 cm (28 in) long. It was one of the earliest-known pterosaurs, which were relatives of dinosaurs. It had skin wings, a long, bony tail, and toothy jaws used for seizing small fish.

Clawed finger

Elongated fourth finger

Armoured back

Front teeth project forwards

Wing made of skin

Bony tail

Beak for cropping plants

Sea reptiles
Placodus ("flat tooth") was as long as a man and belonged to a group of sea reptiles called placodonts. About 200 million years ago, this bulky, short-necked creature plucked shellfish from rocks with its jutting front teeth, then crushed them using flat teeth in the roof of its mouth.

Fossil skull

Sprawling limb

Fur probably covered body

Plant-eating reptiles
Several groups of giant reptiles dominated Triassic wildlife before dinosaurs replaced them. This beaked skull comes from *Hyperodapedon*, a piglike reptile that belonged a group of plant-eating reptiles called rhynchosaurs.

Mammals
During the Triassic Period, mammals evolved from reptilelike ancestors. The small, shrewlike *Megazostrodon* lived in southern Africa and had almost all the features of a mammal. It would have snapped up insects and baby lizards, but kept well clear of hungry dinosaurs.

Mammal-like teeth of different shapes and sizes

Plateosaurus (215 mya)
This European prosauropod grew to 8 m (26 ft) long, but the bulky plant-eater supported itself on its hind limbs only.

Eocursor (210 mya)
A fast-running plant-eater, *Eocursor* is the only Triassic ornithischian for which fairly complete fossils have been found.

Coelophysis (208 mya)
This theropod had slim, pointed jaws and swallowed smaller creatures. Its bones have been found in New Mexico, USA.

Jurassic times

The Jurassic Period lasted from around 200 to 145 million years ago. It is sometimes called the Age of Giants as huge sauropod dinosaurs flourished at this time. By now the continent Pangaea had begun to break into two large landmasses and the Atlantic Ocean had begun to form. Moist ocean winds brought rain to deserts. It was warm everywhere. Plants began to grow in barren lands, providing food for new kinds of dinosaurs. Pterosaurs shared the skies with the first birds. Early salamanders swam in lakes and streams, and Jurassic seas swarmed with big, swimming reptiles.

The Jurassic world
Pangaea broke up into two landmasses called Laurasia and Gondwana. Then Laurasia began splitting into North America, Europe, and Asia, while Gondwana split into South America, Australia, Africa, India, and Antarctica.

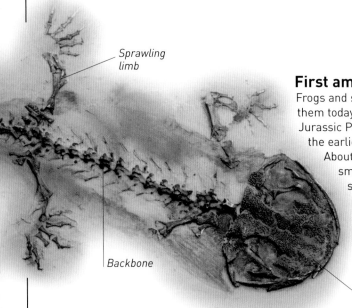

Sprawling limb

Backbone

First amphibians
Frogs and salamanders as we know them today first appeared in the Jurassic Period. *Karaurus* is one of the earliest-known salamanders. About 20 cm (8 in) long, this small amphibian was a good swimmer. It probably lived in streams and pools, snapping up snails and insects.

Broad skull

Jurassic sea reptiles
Apart from its long, narrow jaws and vertical tail, *Ichthyosaurus* was shaped like a dolphin. It grew 2 m (6.5 ft) long and swam at speed. Ichthyosaurs were one of several groups of large Jurassic sea reptiles that were not related to dinosaurs.

Giants and birds
During the Jurassic Period, the prosauropods died out, but sauropods and theropods flourished. Among them were the largest land animals of the time. The ornithopods, stegosaurs, and ankylosaurs all appeared in the Jurassic Period.

Scelidosaurus (190 mya)
The ankylosaur *Scelidosaurus* lived in Laurasia and was one of the earliest and most primitive armoured dinosaurs.

Barapasaurus (190 mya)
The sauropod *Barapasaurus* ("big-legged lizard") gets its name from a thigh bone 1.7 m (5.5 ft) long. It lived in Jurassic India.

Guanlong (160 mya)
Guanlong belonged to the tyrannosauroid group of theropods. This crested dinosaur from China grew only 3 m (10 ft) long.

Long neck

Long skull

Jurassic vegetation
The major Jurassic plants were
those that had flourished in the
Triassic Period. These included
ginkgoes, monkey puzzle trees, and
cycadeoids, such as *Williamsonia* –
a small, stumpy tree with palmlike
leaves. Ferns, horsetails, and mosses
thrived in areas with damp soil.

Leaves of
a monkey
puzzle
tree

Wing made
of skin

Cycadlike
leaves

Williamsonia
plants

Agile fliers
Jurassic pterosaurs, such as
Pterodactylus, had longer necks and
skulls than their Triassic ancestors.
Their short tails made them agile in
the air. Many species of *Pterodactylus*
lived in Africa and Europe, the largest
with a wingspan of 2.4 m (95 in).

Powerful jaws

Crocodile ancestor
Protosuchus ("first crocodile") belonged
to the same group of reptiles as modern
crocodiles and alligators. Only remotely
related to dinosaurs, it had longer legs
and ran about on land. It was the size
of a large dog and lived in Arizona, USA.

Short, stocky trunk

Kentrosaurus (156 mya)
Related to *Stegosaurus*, the African
Kentrosaurus ("spiky lizard") had narrow
plates jutting from its neck, back, and tail.

Sinraptor (155 mya)
Sinraptor lived in what is now a desert in
northwest China. This big meat-eater
grew to about 7.6 m (25 ft) long.

Archaeopteryx (150 mya)
The crow-sized bird *Archaeopteryx* had
feathered wings and body but also had a
theropod's teeth, claws, tail, and scaly legs.

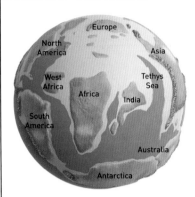

Cretaceous times

The Cretaceous Period lasted from 145 to 65 million years ago and marked the end of the Mesozoic Era. Climates remained warm, but great changes happened to our planet. Flowering plants appeared, lands flooded, and continents moved apart. In the late Cretaceous Period, there were probably more kinds of dinosaur than ever before.

The Cretaceous world

In the Cretaceous Period, Laurasia and Gondwana broke up completely. Their fragments began taking on the shapes and positions of the continents we know today. For a while, shallow seas flowed over stretches of low-lying land.

Upper part of trunk covered with leaves

From foliage to flowers

In the early Cretaceous Period, plants such as conifers and ferns still covered the land. One plant of the time was the tree-fern *Tempskya*, which had a false trunk made of stems. Flowering plants and shrubs began to grow on open ground. By the end of the Cretaceous Period, magnolias and other flowering trees had formed vast forests.

Magnolia flower

Tempskya tree-fern forest

An age of diversity

Cretaceous dinosaurs included some of the most massive sauropods and theropods of all time. Theropods now also included an amazing variety of feathered birds and birdlike dinosaurs. Stegosaurs had vanished, but the horned dinosaurs appeared, as well as the largest ankylosaurs and ornithopods.

Sauropelta (115 mya)

Sauropelta was an ankylosaur that roamed North American woodlands. Bony cones and studs guarded its back and tail.

Alxasaurus (110 mya)

Alxasaurus from China's Alxa Desert was an early therizinosauroid – one of a group of plant-eating theropods.

Styracosaurus (76.5 mya)

A large horned dinosaur from North America, *Styracosaurus* had long spikes on its neck frill and a sharp beak.

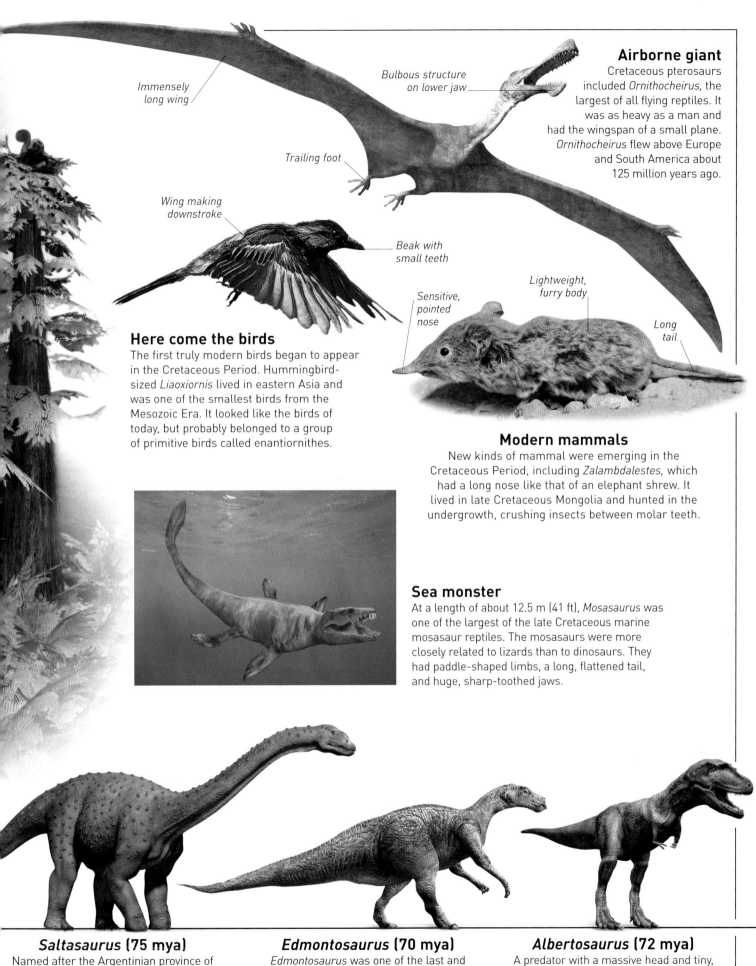

Immensely long wing

Bulbous structure on lower jaw

Trailing foot

Airborne giant
Cretaceous pterosaurs included *Ornithocheirus*, the largest of all flying reptiles. It was as heavy as a man and had the wingspan of a small plane. *Ornithocheirus* flew above Europe and South America about 125 million years ago.

Wing making downstroke

Beak with small teeth

Sensitive, pointed nose

Lightweight, furry body

Long tail

Here come the birds
The first truly modern birds began to appear in the Cretaceous Period. Hummingbird-sized *Liaoxiornis* lived in eastern Asia and was one of the smallest birds from the Mesozoic Era. It looked like the birds of today, but probably belonged to a group of primitive birds called enantiornithes.

Modern mammals
New kinds of mammal were emerging in the Cretaceous Period, including *Zalambdalestes*, which had a long nose like that of an elephant shrew. It lived in late Cretaceous Mongolia and hunted in the undergrowth, crushing insects between molar teeth.

Sea monster
At a length of about 12.5 m (41 ft), *Mosasaurus* was one of the largest of the late Cretaceous marine mosasaur reptiles. The mosasaurs were more closely related to lizards than to dinosaurs. They had paddle-shaped limbs, a long, flattened tail, and huge, sharp-toothed jaws.

Saltasaurus (75 mya)
Named after the Argentinian province of Salta where its fossils were first found, this sauropod had bony lumps on its hide.

Edmontosaurus (70 mya)
Edmontosaurus was one of the last and largest of the hadrosaurs (duck-billed dinosaurs). It grew up to 13 m (43 ft) long.

Albertosaurus (72 mya)
A predator with a massive head and tiny, two-fingered hands, *Albertosaurus* was smaller than its relative *Tyrannosaurus*.

The end of an era

Dinosaurs flourished for more than 160 million years. Then, about 65 million years ago, they all disappeared except for the small theropods that we know as birds. This mass extinction was caused by at least two great disasters: a series of massive volcanic eruptions, followed by an asteroid (a large lump of rock from space) that hit Earth with the force of a nuclear explosion.

Volcanic eruptions
At the end of the Cretaceous Period, volcanic eruptions in central India released vast lava flows and huge quantities of toxic gases. These eruptions led to drastic climate change.

Asteroid impact
About 65 million years ago, a molten asteroid 10 km (6 miles) across crashed into Earth at several thousand kilometres an hour. Huge clouds of dust hid the Sun for months. The whole planet cooled, which led to the extinction of seven out of every ten species of creature that lived on land or at sea.

Fireball striking Earth

Shockwave

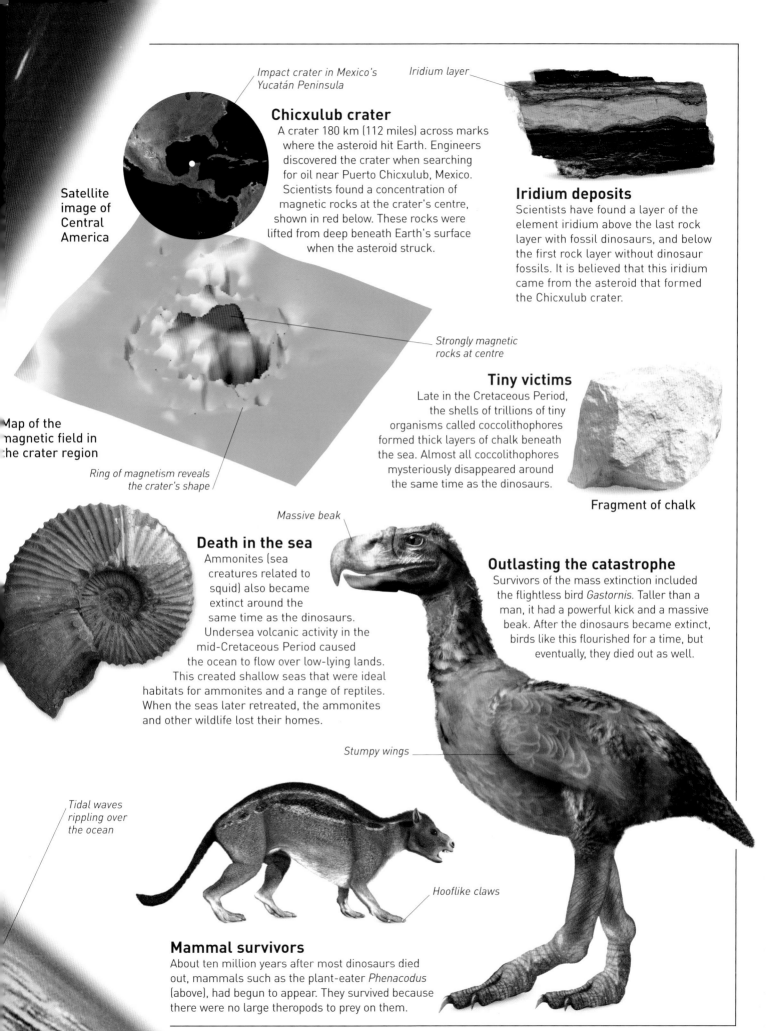

Impact crater in Mexico's Yucatán Peninsula

Iridium layer

Chicxulub crater
A crater 180 km (112 miles) across marks where the asteroid hit Earth. Engineers discovered the crater when searching for oil near Puerto Chicxulub, Mexico. Scientists found a concentration of magnetic rocks at the crater's centre, shown in red below. These rocks were lifted from deep beneath Earth's surface when the asteroid struck.

Satellite image of Central America

Iridium deposits
Scientists have found a layer of the element iridium above the last rock layer with fossil dinosaurs, and below the first rock layer without dinosaur fossils. It is believed that this iridium came from the asteroid that formed the Chicxulub crater.

Strongly magnetic rocks at centre

Map of the magnetic field in the crater region

Ring of magnetism reveals the crater's shape

Tiny victims
Late in the Cretaceous Period, the shells of trillions of tiny organisms called coccolithophores formed thick layers of chalk beneath the sea. Almost all coccolithophores mysteriously disappeared around the same time as the dinosaurs.

Fragment of chalk

Massive beak

Death in the sea
Ammonites (sea creatures related to squid) also became extinct around the same time as the dinosaurs. Undersea volcanic activity in the mid-Cretaceous Period caused the ocean to flow over low-lying lands. This created shallow seas that were ideal habitats for ammonites and a range of reptiles. When the seas later retreated, the ammonites and other wildlife lost their homes.

Outlasting the catastrophe
Survivors of the mass extinction included the flightless bird *Gastornis*. Taller than a man, it had a powerful kick and a massive beak. After the dinosaurs became extinct, birds like this flourished for a time, but eventually, they died out as well.

Stumpy wings

Tidal waves rippling over the ocean

Hooflike claws

Mammal survivors
About ten million years after most dinosaurs died out, mammals such as the plant-eater *Phenacodus* (above), had begun to appear. They survived because there were no large theropods to prey on them.

Limestone

Sandstone

Shale

Volcanic ash

Limestone

Volcanic ash

Shale

Limestone

How do we know?

We know what dinosaurs were like because palaeontologists (scientists who study fossils) have dug up their remains. Fossils are the remains of plants and animals that have turned to rock over millions of years. Usually only fossilized bones are left, although sometimes softer body parts, such as the skin, tendons, and muscles have survived.

Digging up the past
Palaeontologist Luis Chiappe excavates a *Protoceratops* skull in Mongolia's Gobi Desert. Determined dinosaur hunters often work in extremely harsh conditions to excavate fossil bones.

Dinosaur at river bank

Bones of recently dead dinosaurs

Layers building up on to

Stack of layered rocks

Dry river bed

Dinosaur fossil

Rock layers
Fossils occur in sedimentary rocks, which are formed when sand, mud, and gravel build up in layers over many millions of years. A series of rock layers can be seen in a cliff face (as shown here). The oldest rocks lie at the bottom and the youngest at the top. Index fossils are fossils that belong to a particular period, and help to date the rocks. Ammonites, for example, are index fossils for the Mesozoic Era.

The story of a fossil
These block diagrams tell the story of dinosaurs that drowned in a river. Their bones were buried in layers of mud that slowly turned into rock. Minerals seeping into pores in the bones changed them into fossils. Over millions of years, wind and rain wore away the rocks, leaving the fossils exposed.

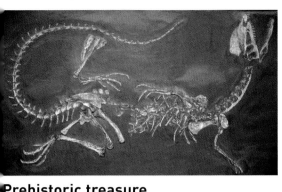

Prehistoric treasure

Almost all the bones in this *Dilophosaurus* skeleton are still intact and most are connected to each other. Fossil dinosaur skeletons as complete as this are extremely rare. Dinosaur hunters are more likely to find tiny, isolated scraps of bone that were scattered by scavenging animals or the weather.

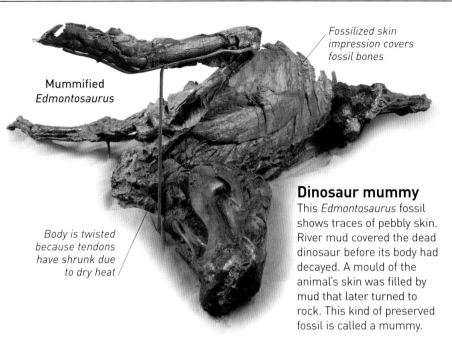

Mummified *Edmontosaurus*

Fossilized skin impression covers fossil bones

Body is twisted because tendons have shrunk due to dry heat

Dinosaur mummy

This *Edmontosaurus* fossil shows traces of pebbly skin. River mud covered the dead dinosaur before its body had decayed. A mould of the animal's skin was filled by mud that later turned to rock. This kind of preserved fossil is called a mummy.

Moulds and casts

Sometimes a dead organism rots away, leaving its impression in the mud. This kind of fossil is called a mould. As the mud turns into rock, minerals seep into the impression and form a stony lump in the shape of the organism. These fossils are called casts.

Impression of the organism

Ammonite mould

Ammonite cast

Stony lump in the shape of the organism

Palaeontologist excavating a dinosaur fossil

Eroded desert

Trace fossils

A footprint shows where a dinosaur once walked through mud that later hardened into rock. Fossil eggs, nests, and dung also reveal how the living dinosaurs behaved. These fossilized signs, or traces, of an animal (rather than fossils of the animal itself) are known as trace fossils.

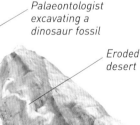

Frond-shaped carbon film

Carbonized plant

A shiny black and brown film made of carbon is all that remains of this fern frond preserved in a rock. Plant fossils help scientists to work out what the vegetation was like in a particular place at a particular time.

Megalosaurus thigh bone

The first fossil finds

In 1820, a British doctor named Gideon Mantell began collecting large fossilized bones and teeth dug up in a Sussex quarry. He believed they came from a giant prehistoric reptile, which he named *Iguanodon*. Soon, the bones of two more monstrous animals came to light. The British scientist Richard Owen claimed all three belonged to a single group of reptiles, for which he invented the term Dinosauria, meaning "terrible lizards".

An early find
The first picture of a dinosaur fossil was published in 1677 in a book by Robert Plot, an English museum curator. Plot mistook the fossil for a thigh bone of a giant man.

A toothy clue
Gideon Mantell (1790–1852) noticed that large fossil teeth like this one resembled the smaller teeth of an iguana lizard. So he used the name *Iguanodon*, meaning "iguana toothed". The tooth was probably found by local quarrymen, who were paid by Mantell to look for fossil bones.

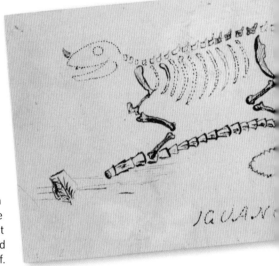

Guess again!
Mantell drew this sketch to show what he believed *Iguanodon* looked like. It was largely guesswork based on a few broken bones. The animal resembles a large iguana lizard. Mantell mistakenly thought a thumb spike was a horn on the creature's nose. He also thought that its tail was whiplike, instead of being heavy and stiff.

The first of many
In 1824, British geologist William Buckland (1784–1856) published his description of the *Megalosaurus* fossil jaw. This was the first dinosaur to get a scientific name. Although Mantell had named *Iguanodon* by 1822, he only put its name in print in 1825.

Sharp, serrated tooth

Dentary (bone in lower jaw)

Megalosaurus jaw

What's in a name?

This cartoon is of Richard Owen (1804–1892), an expert in anatomy who suggested the term "dinosaur". Owen realized that dinosaurs formed a special group because, unlike ordinary reptiles, they stood on erect limbs, and their backbones above the hips were fused (joined) together.

Lifesize sculptures

The earliest lifesize models of dinosaurs resembled scaly, reptilian rhinoceroses. Advised by Richard Owen, sculptor Benjamin Waterhouse Hawkins made concrete models of *Iguanodon*, *Megalosaurus*, and *Hylaeosaurus* and placed them in an artificial lake in Sydenham Park in London, in 1853.

Concrete *Iguanodon* models

Long front tooth

Wild, wild west

Bones of the mini-sauropod *Anchisaurus* had apparently been unearthed in Connecticut, USA, as early as 1818. In the 1870s, palaeontologists began finding dinosaur fossils in quarries in the American Wild West. This photograph shows the famous US dinosaur hunter Barnum Brown (1873–1963) examining huge bones at a quarry in Wyoming, USA, in 1941. His earlier finds included the first *Tyrannosaurus* skeleton, dug up in Montana in 1902.

Fact or fiction?

The earliest dinosaur discoveries may date back more than 2,600 years. People in central Asia spoke of a creature with a hooked beak and talon-tipped limbs. This mythical beast may have been inspired by a beaked dinosaur called *Protoceratops*, whose fossils have been found in central Asia. The stories seem to have reached Persia (modern Iran), where people carved images of the beast.

Persian statue of a griffin

Little and large

Although many people think of dinosaurs as giant beasts, most were no bigger than an elephant. However, some sauropods did become the largest creatures ever to walk on land. Built like a giant giraffe, *Brachiosaurus* stood as high as a four-storey building. *Diplodocus* grew up to 33.5 m (110 ft). Perhaps the largest of all was North America's *Amphicoelias*. Sadly, scientists found only part of one of its back bones, then lost it. In contrast, the theropod *Compsognathus* was little bigger than a chicken, and the birdlike *Microraptor* was smaller still.

The high life
A mounted *Barosaurus* skeleton in the American Museum of Natural History gives visitors an idea of the creature's awesome size. The head of this female *Barosaurus* is 15.2 m (50 ft) above the ground.

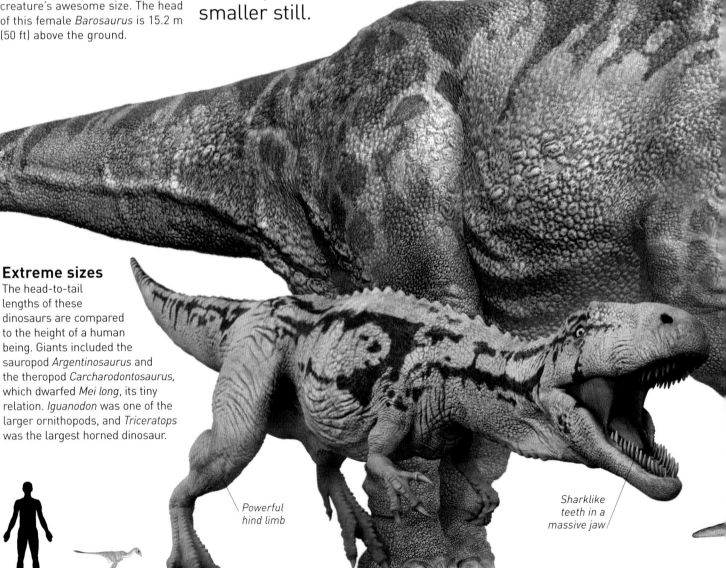

Extreme sizes
The head-to-tail lengths of these dinosaurs are compared to the height of a human being. Giants included the sauropod *Argentinosaurus* and the theropod *Carcharodontosaurus*, which dwarfed *Mei long*, its tiny relation. *Iguanodon* was one of the larger ornithopods, and *Triceratops* was the largest horned dinosaur.

Powerful hind limb

Sharklike teeth in a massive jaw

Human	Mei long	Carcharodontosaurus	Argentinosaurus
1.8 m (6 ft)	68.5 cm (27 in)	13.5 m (44 ft)	30.5–33.5 m (100–110 ft)

Movie monsters

The huge size of some dinosaurs has inspired a host of movie characters, such as Godzilla. Scientists know that no dinosaurs ever grew this large, but special effects have created impossibly large creatures that look quite real.

Godzilla terrorizes the streets of New York City, USA

Small head relative to body size

Clawed finger

Dinosaur biplane

Microraptor gui was one of the smallest non-bird dinosaurs. It measured about 77 cm (30 in) in length and weighed only 1 kg (2.2 lb). This little theropod was capable of gliding at least 40 m (130 ft) from tree to tree.

Feathered legs served as extra wings

Long neck

Compsognathus

Birdlike foot

Chicken

Chicken-sized

Compsognathus was once known as the smallest dinosaur. Scientists discovered that it preyed on lizards when they found the remains of the lizard *Bavarisaurus* in the ribcage of a fossilized *Compsognathus*.

Head could be lifted to about 5 m (16.5 ft) above ground when rearing

Iguanodon
11 m (36 ft)

Triceratops
9 m (29.5 ft)

Evolution

Fishy forerunner

Panderichthys was a fish that lived about 380 million years ago. A fish like this was the ancestor of all tetrapods (four-legged, backboned animals). Its fins were supported by bones like those found in our limbs, and its skull and ribs were more like those of tetrapods than fish.

Both dinosaurs and humans evolved from the same prehistoric backboned animal. Evolution is the process by which a species gradually adapts to its changing environment. Over many years, new species are formed. Those species that don't adapt die out. Four-legged animals evolved from a fish with fins. One group of these four-legged animals became our mammal ancestors. Another group evolved into reptiles, and some reptiles evolved into dinosaurs.

Paddlelike tail fin

Acanthostega

Eight digits

The first creatures with legs

Acanthostega was one of the earliest tetrapods and one of the first vertebrates (backboned animals) with limbs. It lived in shallow water around 360 million years ago, and had features found in both fish and tetrapods. Like fish, it had gills and a tail fin – and like most tetrapods, it had hip bones, limb bones, and toes, which allowed it to walk.

Westlothiana

Five digits

Ancestors of reptiles

The eggs of early tetrapods needed to be laid in water to prevent them from drying out. Then some tetrapods, such as *Westlothiana*, began producing eggs protected by a membrane called an amnion. This allowed them to breed on land. These animals, known as amniotes, were the ancestors of reptiles and mammals.

Lizardlike tail

Sprawling leg

Chasmatosaurus

A sprawling walker

Chasmatosaurus belonged to a group of reptiles called archosaurs, which also included crocodiles and dinosaurs. With limbs that stuck out sideways, *Chasmatosaurus* walked in a sprawling way.

Euparkeria

Leg tucked in

Rearing to run

Agile archosaurs, such as the cat-sized *Euparkeria*, were the descendants of the early, sprawling reptiles. *Euparkeria* lived about 245 million years ago. It walked on all fours, but probably reared to run on its hind limbs, using its tail for balance.

Skeletons compared
The skeletons of this *Tyrannosaurus* and human almost match bone for bone because they both evolved from the same fishy ancestor. The main difference is in the number and proportion of some bones. *Tyrannosaurus* has a longer skull. The dinosaur has enough vertebrae to form a long tail, while humans have one tail bone, known as the coccyx.

Tyrannosaurus skeleton labels:
- Pelvis (hip bone)
- Dorsal vertebra (back bone)
- Skull
- Caudal vertebra (tail bone)
- Rib
- Manus (hand)
- Tibia (shin bone)
- Phalanx (toe bone)

Tyrannosaurus skeleton

Human skeleton labels:
- Skull
- Vertebra
- Manus (hand)
- Coccyx (tail bone)
- Rib
- Pelvis (hip bone)
- Phalanx (toe bone)
- Tibia (shin bone)

Human skeleton

Dinosaur dawn
One of the earliest dinosaurs was *Eoraptor*, which lived 228 million years ago. Like all theropods, this two-legged hunter had erect legs and grasping hands for seizing prey. But its neck and thumbs were relatively shorter than those of other theropods.

Eoraptor

Heads and brains

A dinosaur's skull was made up of separate bones that slotted together to support the jaws and protect the brain. There were holes for eyes, ears, nostrils, and jaw muscles, and often extra holes to save weight. Dinosaur brains were relatively smaller and less complex than those of most mammals. Some theropods had brains as large as those in certain modern birds. These dinosaurs probably had very keen senses.

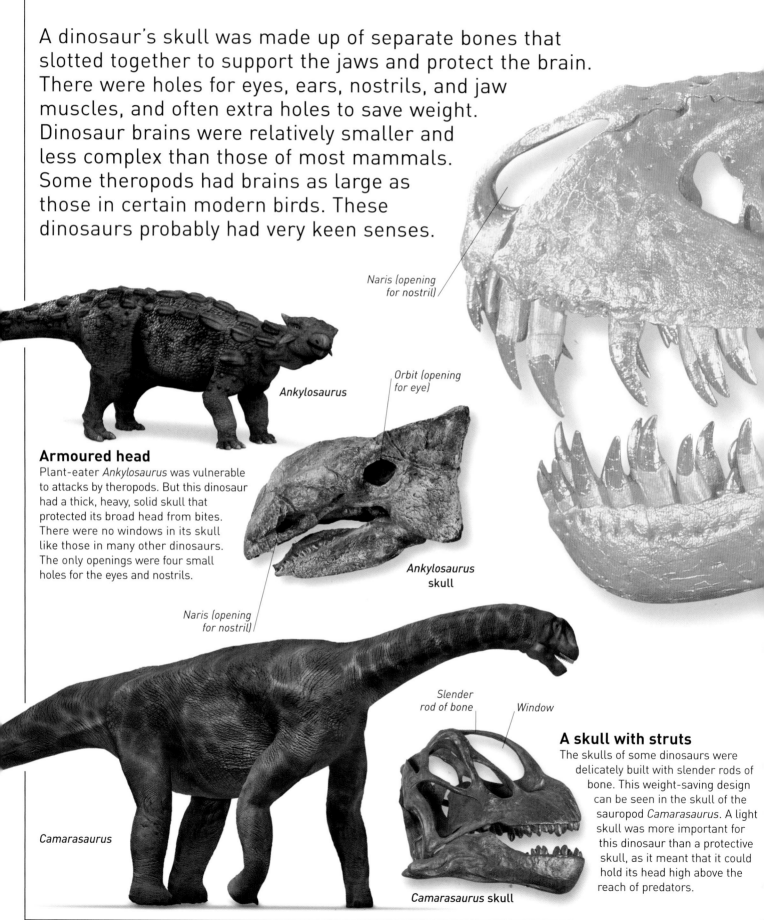

Naris (opening for nostril)

Ankylosaurus

Orbit (opening for eye)

Armoured head

Plant-eater *Ankylosaurus* was vulnerable to attacks by theropods. But this dinosaur had a thick, heavy, solid skull that protected its broad head from bites. There were no windows in its skull like those in many other dinosaurs. The only openings were four small holes for the eyes and nostrils.

Naris (opening for nostril)

Ankylosaurus skull

Slender rod of bone

Window

A skull with struts

The skulls of some dinosaurs were delicately built with slender rods of bone. This weight-saving design can be seen in the skull of the sauropod *Camarasaurus*. A light skull was more important for this dinosaur than a protective skull, as it meant that it could hold its head high above the reach of predators.

Camarasaurus

Camarasaurus skull

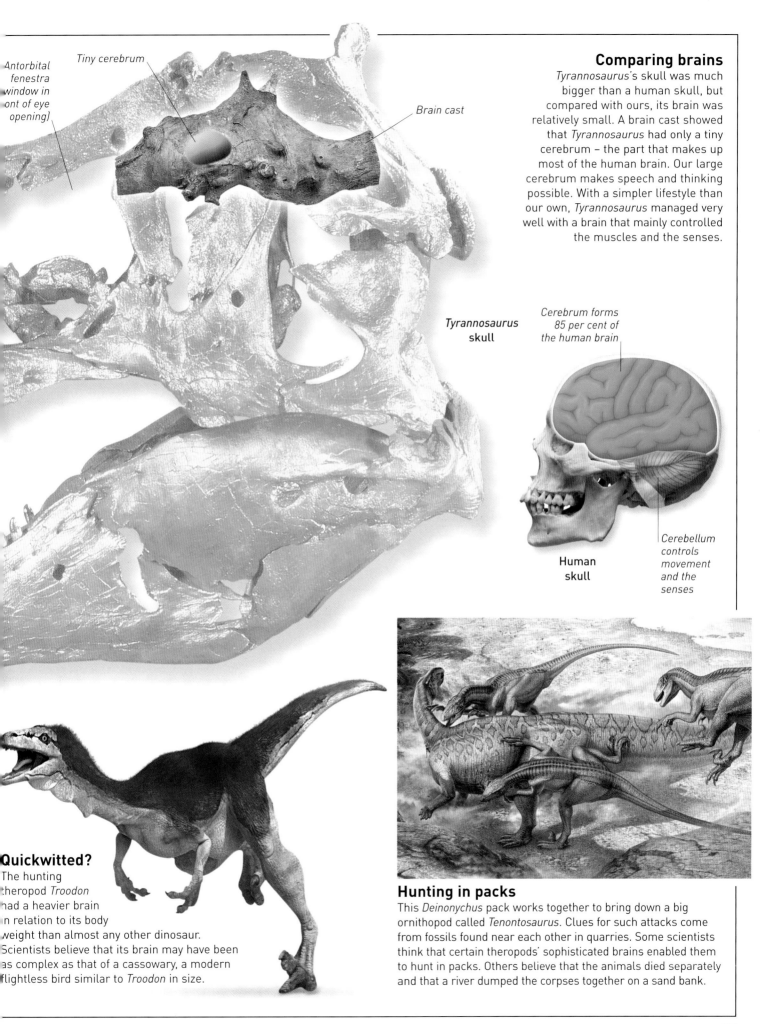

Antorbital
fenestra
(window in
front of eye
opening)

Tiny cerebrum

Brain cast

Comparing brains

Tyrannosaurus's skull was much bigger than a human skull, but compared with ours, its brain was relatively small. A brain cast showed that *Tyrannosaurus* had only a tiny cerebrum – the part that makes up most of the human brain. Our large cerebrum makes speech and thinking possible. With a simpler lifestyle than our own, *Tyrannosaurus* managed very well with a brain that mainly controlled the muscles and the senses.

Tyrannosaurus skull

Cerebrum forms 85 per cent of the human brain

Human skull

Cerebellum controls movement and the senses

Quickwitted?

The hunting theropod *Troodon* had a heavier brain in relation to its body weight than almost any other dinosaur. Scientists believe that its brain may have been as complex as that of a cassowary, a modern flightless bird similar to *Troodon* in size.

Hunting in packs

This *Deinonychus* pack works together to bring down a big ornithopod called *Tenontosaurus*. Clues for such attacks come from fossils found near each other in quarries. Some scientists think that certain theropods' sophisticated brains enabled them to hunt in packs. Others believe that the animals died separately and that a river dumped the corpses together on a sand bank.

Horns and crests

The skulls of many dinosaurs had bumps, horns, or head crests. These were probably used for display – to scare a rival or to impress a mate – or to help other dinosaurs to spot members of their species from a distance. Skulls with sturdy bumps and horns could have served as weapons of attack. But perhaps the most effective use of bumps, crests, and horns was to frighten off enemies or predators.

Three-horned face

Two brow horns 1 m (3.3 ft) long and a short nose horn earned *Triceratops* its name, which means "three-horned face". Males probably used their horns as weapons or to ward off attack. The bony shield at the back of the head saved their necks from injury.

Long brow horn

Small nose horn

A thick nose

Instead of the sharp nose horn of most large plant-eating ceratopsians, the North American *Pachyrhinosaurus* ("thick-nosed lizard") grew a bony lump that was broad and flattish. Some dinosaur lumps dipped in the middle, while others bulged. Rival males probably used these bumps to push each other until the weaker male gave way.

Helmet-shaped skull roof

Narrow beak

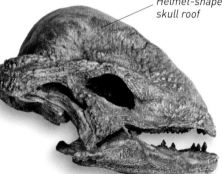

Thick-headed

Pachycephalosaurs ("thick-headed lizards") such as *Stegoceras* had very thick skull roofs. These domes were used to protect the brains during attack or to frighten off rivals. Many animals today use horns or fangs in this way instead of risking injury by fighting.

Ready to fight

Each autumn, rival male deer use their antlers to threaten each other. Two evenly matched stags will lock antlers and try to shove each other backwards. The winner earns the right to mate with many females. It is likely that some horned dinosaurs behaved in a similar way.

Shield-shaped
back of skull

Horn jutting from
above the eyes

Short snout

Sharp teeth

Bull's horns

Two cowlike horns stuck out sideways from the head of *Carnotaurus*. Unlike the horns of other predatory dinosaurs, these horns were too short and stubby to help this theropod kill its prey and might have served as an ornament to attract a mate. However, a pair of duelling males could have used their horns as weapons, by swinging their heads at each other's necks.

Lambeosaurus

Corythosaurus

Crested dinosaurs

Tall, narrow crests crowned the heads of some hadrosaurs (duck-billed dinosaurs). *Lambeosaurus* had a tall, bonnet-shaped crest, and *Corythosaurus* ("helmet lizard") sported a head crest shaped like half a dinner plate. Crests probably helped a dinosaur to recognize others of its kind.

Senses

Dinosaurs depended on sight, smell, taste, hearing, balance, and touch to find food and mates, and to detect danger. Although organs like eyes rarely fossilized, scientists can tell from holes in a dinosaur's skull how large its eyes were and which way they faced. A dinosaur's braincase can also show whether its brain had large, complex areas to deal with hearing and smell. Many dinosaurs had senses as acute as those of many animals living today.

Long, tubelike crest made of nose bones

Calling out
To communicate with other herd members, *Parasaurolophus* tooted like a trombone by forcing air out through its hollow head crest. Hadrosaurs without head crests probably blew up skin flaps on their faces, much as frogs croak by inflating their throat pouches.

Eye facing right

Gallimimus

Side vision
Like a horse, the ostrichlike dinosaur *Gallimimus* had an eye on each side of its head – one looked left and the other looked right. Each eye saw things the other could not. Between them, the two eyes could spot a predator creeping up from behind. This gave *Gallimimus* time to dash away before being caught.

Troodon

Eyes forward
Troodon had large, forward-facing eyes that could see and focus on the same thing at once, such as baby hadrosaur prey. The eyes produced a three-dimensional image of the prey in *Troodon*'s brain, and enabled the theropod to judge the distance between itself and its victim.

Seeing things
The areas in blue show how much of the world *Gallimimus* and *Troodon* could see. *Gallimimus* had a much wider field of vision than *Troodon*, but *Troodon* could judge distances better directly in front.

Narrow field of overlapping vision

Field of vision of left eye

Field of vision of right eye

Gallimimus's field of vision

Wide field of overlapping vision

Field of vision of left eye

Field of vision of right eye

Troodon's field of vision

Large eye with good nocturnal (night) vision

Eye facing forwards

In the dark
The ornithopod _Leaellynasaura_ had big optic lobes – parts of the brain that interpret what the eyes see. This meant that it probably had good night vision, which helped it to survive the long, dark winters. It lived in southern Australia about 110 million years ago – a time when that part of the world lay close to Earth's south pole and was covered in darkness in winter.

Sniffing it out
Tyrannosaurus ("tyrant lizard") had large olfactory lobes – parts of the brain that interpret what the nose smells. This suggests that this Cretaceous theropod had a keen sense of smell. Like a turkey vulture, it could probably smell a dead body lying nearly 1 km (0.6 miles) away.

Head crest

Bright and colourful
Bright colours might have adorned the head crest of _Cryolophosaurus_ ("frozen crested lizard"), a large theropod found in an icy Antarctic mountain. Colourful skin, crests, or feathers were probably used to help male theropods attract mates.

Hiding in plain sight
Standing among tree ferns, a greenish _Iguanodon_ would have been almost invisible to its predators. No one knows what this animal's skin colour really was, but many dinosaurs were probably coloured or patterned with spots or stripes so that they matched their surroundings.

Meat-eaters

Many large meat-eating dinosaurs, such as *Allosaurus*, had powerful jaws and knifelike teeth for killing and tearing up prey. But not all theropods had heads for tackling such heavy tasks. Spinosaurids were shaped for seizing fish, and small sharp-toothed coelurosaurs swallowed lizards whole. Beaked ornithomimids were toothless and snapped up insects, but also fed on plants.

Serrated edge

Cracks due to fossilization

New tooth

Killing teeth

With serrated edges like a knife, the curved teeth of *Megalosaurus* sliced easily through flesh and crunched through bone. Such use made them wear out quickly, but new teeth always grew to replace those that were worn out or lost.

Large, curved tooth of *Megalosaurus*

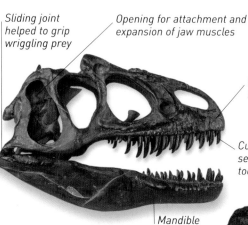

Sliding joint helped to grip wriggling prey

Opening for attachment and expansion of jaw muscles

Maxilla (upper jaw)

Curved, serrated tooth

Mandible (lower jaw)

Top chopper

Sturdy bones in *Allosaurus*'s skull supported its jaw and bladelike teeth. It would snap its jaws on a victim then slice off flesh with its sharp teeth. Its skull was designed to rapidly chop flesh, unlike the bone-crushing skull of *Tyrannosaurus*.

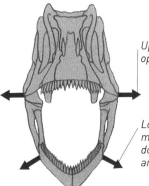

Upper jaw opens far apart

Lower jaw moves downwards and outwards

Open wide

Movable joints between some of the bones in *Allosaurus*'s skull meant that the jaws could not only gape wide apart, but could expand outwards to engulf huge chunks of meat.

Tarbosaurus

Barsboldia

Tyrannosaur attack

This *Tarbosaurus* has clamped its powerful jaws on the neck of a young *Barsboldia*. Both dinosaurs lived in the eastern part of central Asia. *Tarbosaurus* grew nearly as huge as its American cousin *Tyrannosaurus*, and probably preyed on hadrosaur herds. Too slow to catch big or fit animals, *Tarbosaurus* preyed on the sick, old, and young.

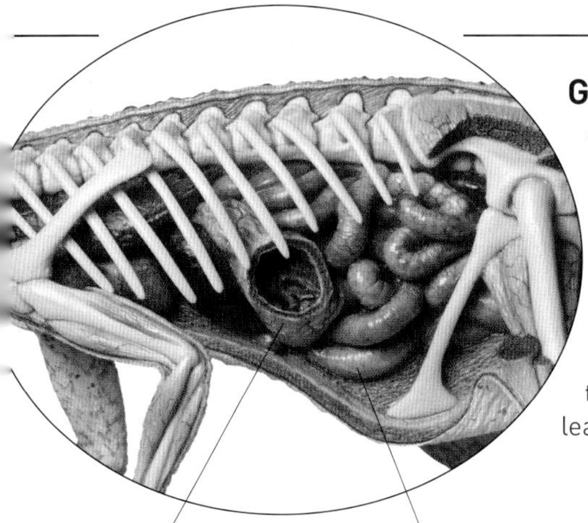

Gut and gizzard

A theropod's digestive juices dissolved meat and even bones inside the gut. The dinosaur may have swallowed bones to help break up food in a muscular organ called the gizzard. Meat has less fibre than plants, making it easier to digest (break down) than leafy vegetation.

Gizzard

Intestine

Bone fragments of prey

Dinosaur droppings

Scientists study the fossil droppings of large theropods to discover which animals they ate. They look for undigested scraps of bones and compare slices of these bones with those of known types of dinosaur. This tyrannosaur dropping contains the remains of either a horned or a duck-billed dinosaur.

Muscular back

Balancing tail

Long jaws

Slender tooth

Fish-eater

Baryonyx belonged to a group of fish-eating dinosaurs called spinosaurids. Its slim, pointed teeth were superbly shaped to grip large, wriggling fish. Scientists even found a fossil of a big fish in the ribcage of one *Baryonyx* fossil.

Strong leg

Bony prong

A toothless hunter

Citipati belongs to a group of theropods called oviraptorosaurs. Its strong jaws ended in a toothless beak, but two sharp, bony prongs stuck out from the roof of its mouth. These may have helped it to smash swallowed eggs.

Plant-eaters

Square jaw

The jaws, teeth, stomach, and gut of plant-eating dinosaurs were made for cropping, chewing, and digesting vegetation. Sauropods stripped twigs with teeth shaped like spoons or pencils. Horned dinosaurs chewed tough vegetation with their sharp cheek teeth. Hadrosaurs cropped leaves with their toothless beaks. Most ornithischians probably had fleshy cheeks to hold food while chewing. All of these dinosaurs had long intestines to digest large amounts of plant food.

Numerous teeth

Mowing machine

Nigersaurus had more teeth than any other sauropod. Its lower jaw alone had 68 teeth, and behind each pencil-shaped front tooth, new teeth grew to replace those that were lost. With its square jaw, short-necked *Nigersaurus* cropped low-growing plants like a living lawnmower.

Small intestine

Sauropod digestion

Leaves swallowed by a sauropod passed through its long intestine where they were broken down into simple substances that could be carried around the body. Sauropod ancestors walked on their hind limbs, but over time, sauropods began to walk on all fours because their guts were too heavy to carry in front.

Stones in the gut

Smooth stones found in the remains of certain sauropods led some palaeontologists to believe that the dinosaurs swallowed them to grind food. Sauropods may have had a gizzard (muscular organ for grinding food) like a bird's. But scientists now think that the sauropods swallowed stones either by accident, or deliberately for their nourishing minerals.

Gizzard

Large intestine

Sharp edge of new tooth helped in shredding leaves

Tooth worn down by eating plants

Wear and tear

Two *Iguanodon* cheek teeth – one new, one worn – show the effects of chewing tough plants. Each time *Iguanodon* closed its mouth to grind the leaves, the two side rows of upper teeth slid across the surface of the lower teeth. This kept the teeth sharp but also wore them down.

Iguanodon teeth

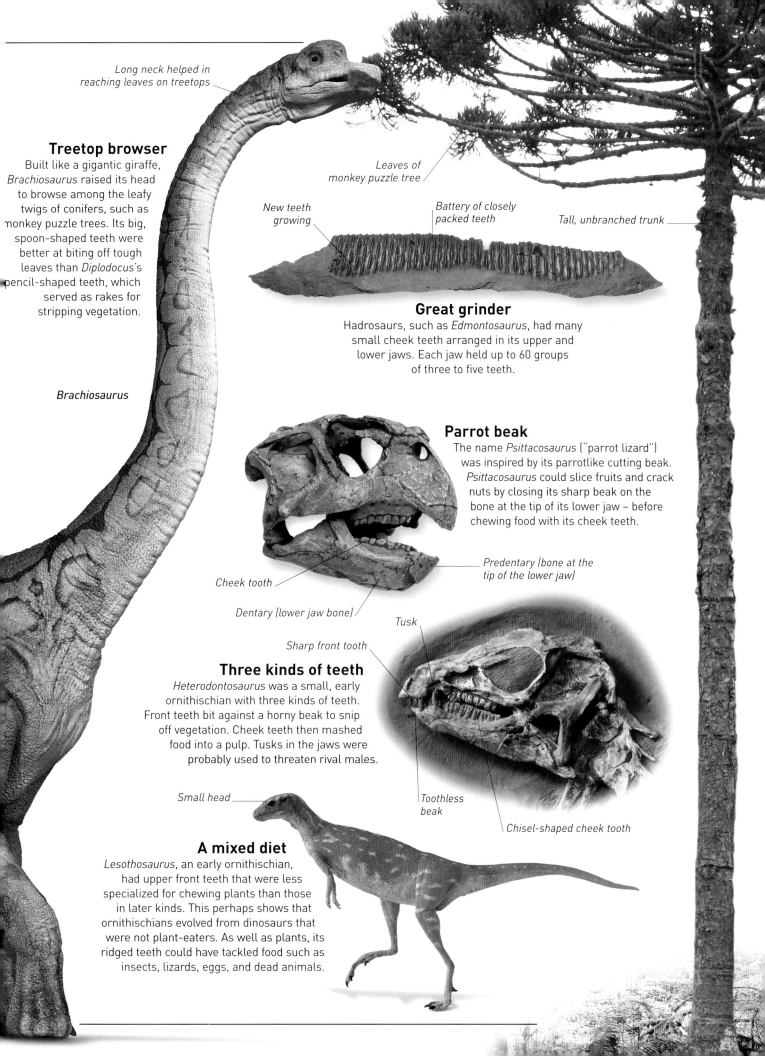

Treetop browser

Built like a gigantic giraffe, *Brachiosaurus* raised its head to browse among the leafy twigs of conifers, such as monkey puzzle trees. Its big, spoon-shaped teeth were better at biting off tough leaves than *Diplodocus*'s pencil-shaped teeth, which served as rakes for stripping vegetation.

Long neck helped in reaching leaves on treetops

Brachiosaurus

Leaves of monkey puzzle tree

New teeth growing

Battery of closely packed teeth

Tall, unbranched trunk

Great grinder

Hadrosaurs, such as *Edmontosaurus*, had many small cheek teeth arranged in its upper and lower jaws. Each jaw held up to 60 groups of three to five teeth.

Parrot beak

The name *Psittacosaurus* ("parrot lizard") was inspired by its parrotlike cutting beak. *Psittacosaurus* could slice fruits and crack nuts by closing its sharp beak on the bone at the tip of its lower jaw – before chewing food with its cheek teeth.

Predentary (bone at the tip of the lower jaw)

Cheek tooth

Dentary (lower jaw bone)

Tusk

Sharp front tooth

Three kinds of teeth

Heterodontosaurus was a small, early ornithischian with three kinds of teeth. Front teeth bit against a horny beak to snip off vegetation. Cheek teeth then mashed food into a pulp. Tusks in the jaws were probably used to threaten rival males.

Small head

Toothless beak

Chisel-shaped cheek tooth

A mixed diet

Lesothosaurus, an early ornithischian, had upper front teeth that were less specialized for chewing plants than those in later kinds. This perhaps shows that ornithischians evolved from dinosaurs that were not plant-eaters. As well as plants, its ridged teeth could have tackled food such as insects, lizards, eggs, and dead animals.

Long and short necks

Sauropods had the longest necks of all dinosaurs – some more than five times as long as a giraffe's. In contrast, most armoured, plated, and horned dinosaurs had short, strong necks, and generally fed on vegetation near the ground. Large meat-eaters, such as *Tyrannosaurus*, had massive necks, while smaller theropods, such as *Velociraptor*, had slim necks that uncoiled like springs when attacking prey.

Cervical vertebra (neck bone)

Mandible (lower jaw)

Muscles running along the topside of the neck

Braced for heady heights

Powerful neck muscles lifted *Brachiosaurus*'s head, and a strong heart pumped blood up to its brain. This sauropod's neck was supported at the base in the same way that the movable jib (arm) of a crane is supported by a tower and base. All sauropod necks needed bracing, which came from the muscles, tendons, and the cablelike ligament above the neck bones. Bracing strengthened sauropod necks so that they could work like flexible rods.

Crane with movable jib

Head lifted to about 13 m (43 ft) above ground

Jurassic giants

A *Brachiosaurus* herd would have wandered through riverside forests of conifers, cycads, and ferns. These great sauropods lowered their necks to drink and graze at ground level, and lifted them to feed on treetop leaves. To reach the treetops, these huge creatures might have had to raise their heads to the height of a four-storey office building.

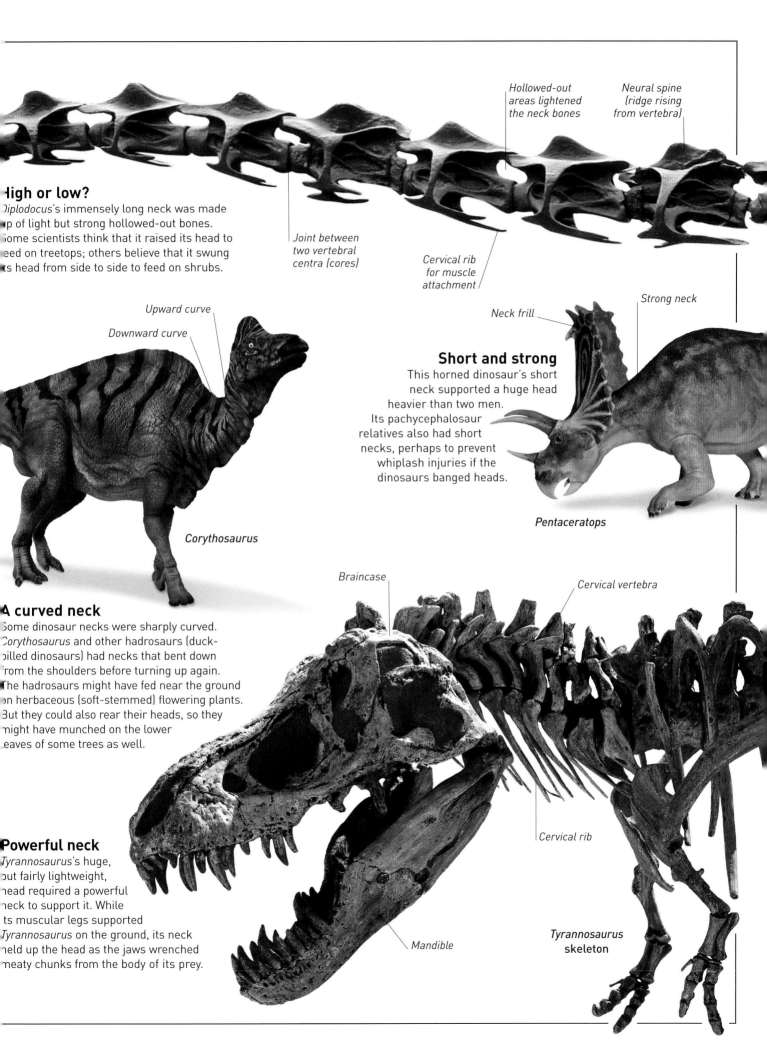

Hollowed-out areas lightened the neck bones

Neural spine (ridge rising from vertebra)

High or low?

Diplodocus's immensely long neck was made up of light but strong hollowed-out bones. Some scientists think that it raised its head to feed on treetops; others believe that it swung its head from side to side to feed on shrubs.

Joint between two vertebral centra (cores)

Cervical rib for muscle attachment

Upward curve

Downward curve

Neck frill

Strong neck

Short and strong

This horned dinosaur's short neck supported a huge head heavier than two men. Its pachycephalosaur relatives also had short necks, perhaps to prevent whiplash injuries if the dinosaurs banged heads.

Corythosaurus

Pentaceratops

A curved neck

Some dinosaur necks were sharply curved. *Corythosaurus* and other hadrosaurs (duck-billed dinosaurs) had necks that bent down from the shoulders before turning up again. The hadrosaurs might have fed near the ground on herbaceous (soft-stemmed) flowering plants. But they could also rear their heads, so they might have munched on the lower leaves of some trees as well.

Braincase

Cervical vertebra

Cervical rib

Powerful neck

Tyrannosaurus's huge, but fairly lightweight, head required a powerful neck to support it. While its muscular legs supported *Tyrannosaurus* on the ground, its neck held up the head as the jaws wrenched meaty chunks from the body of its prey.

Mandible

Tyrannosaurus skeleton

The backbone story

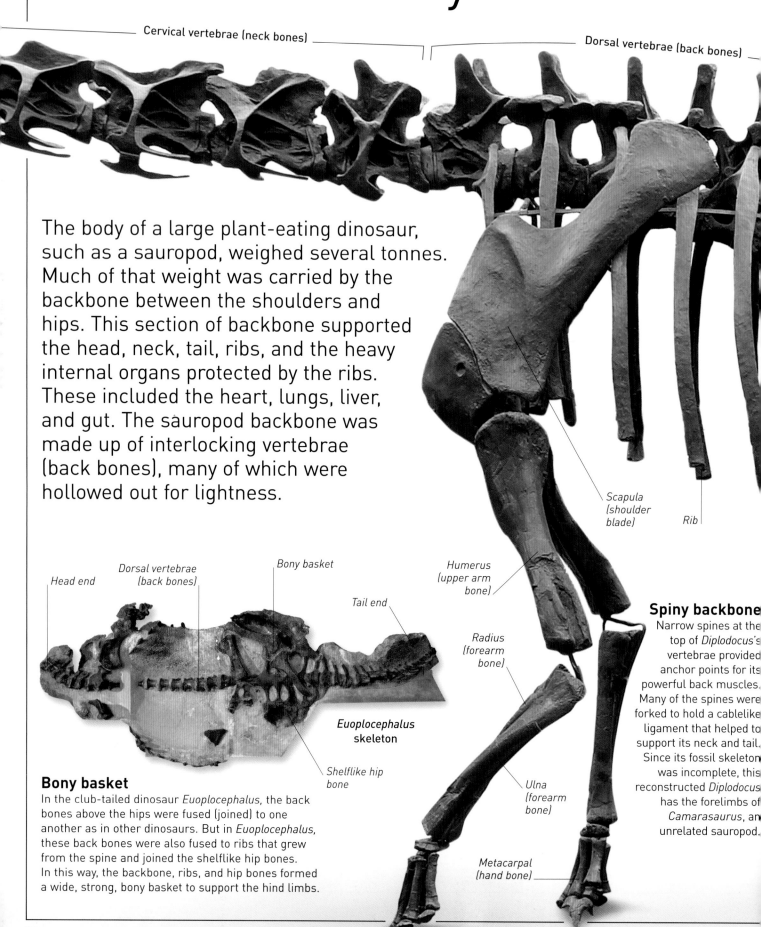

Cervical vertebrae (neck bones)

Dorsal vertebrae (back bones)

The body of a large plant-eating dinosaur, such as a sauropod, weighed several tonnes. Much of that weight was carried by the backbone between the shoulders and hips. This section of backbone supported the head, neck, tail, ribs, and the heavy internal organs protected by the ribs. These included the heart, lungs, liver, and gut. The sauropod backbone was made up of interlocking vertebrae (back bones), many of which were hollowed out for lightness.

Scapula (shoulder blade)

Rib

Head end

Dorsal vertebrae (back bones)

Bony basket

Tail end

Humerus (upper arm bone)

Radius (forearm bone)

Euoplocephalus skeleton

Shelflike hip bone

Ulna (forearm bone)

Bony basket
In the club-tailed dinosaur *Euoplocephalus*, the back bones above the hips were fused (joined) to one another as in other dinosaurs. But in *Euoplocephalus*, these back bones were also fused to ribs that grew from the spine and joined the shelflike hip bones. In this way, the backbone, ribs, and hip bones formed a wide, strong, bony basket to support the hind limbs.

Metacarpal (hand bone)

Spiny backbone
Narrow spines at the top of *Diplodocus*'s vertebrae provided anchor points for its powerful back muscles. Many of the spines were forked to hold a cablelike ligament that helped to support its neck and tail. Since its fossil skeleton was incomplete, this reconstructed *Diplodocus* has the forelimbs of *Camarasaurus*, an unrelated sauropod.

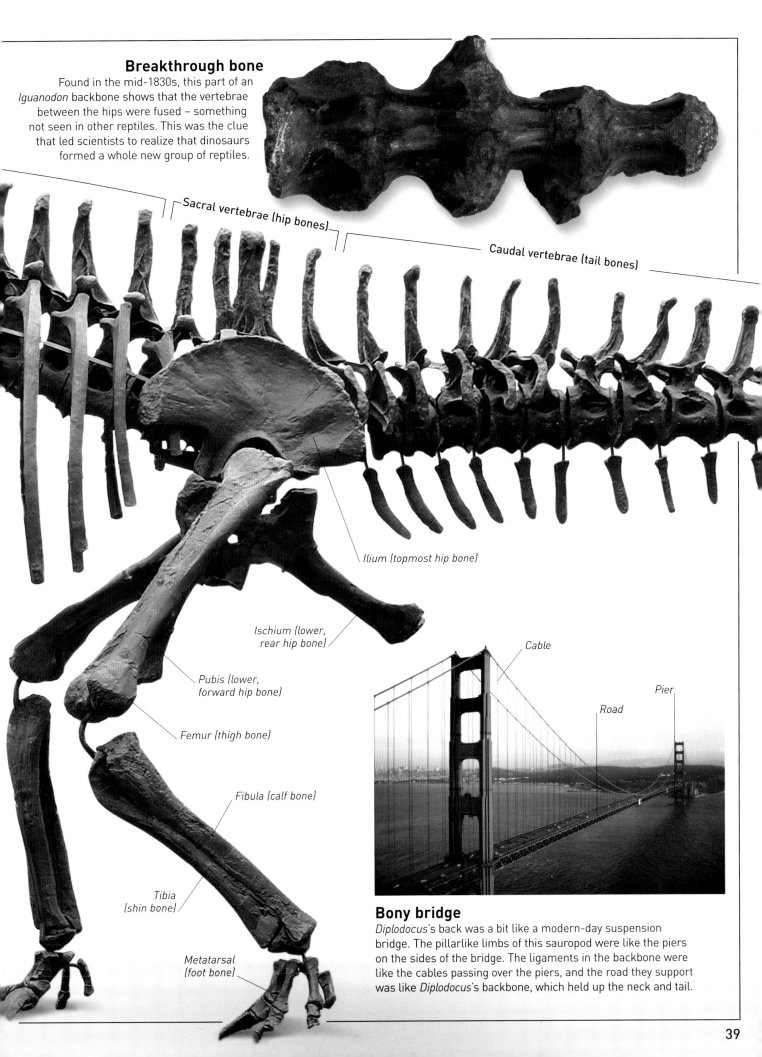

Breakthrough bone
Found in the mid-1830s, this part of an *Iguanodon* backbone shows that the vertebrae between the hips were fused – something not seen in other reptiles. This was the clue that led scientists to realize that dinosaurs formed a whole new group of reptiles.

Sacral vertebrae (hip bones)

Caudal vertebrae (tail bones)

Ilium (topmost hip bone)

Ischium (lower, rear hip bone)

Pubis (lower, forward hip bone)

Femur (thigh bone)

Fibula (calf bone)

Tibia (shin bone)

Metatarsal (foot bone)

Cable

Road

Pier

Bony bridge
Diplodocus's back was a bit like a modern-day suspension bridge. The pillarlike limbs of this sauropod were like the piers on the sides of the bridge. The ligaments in the backbone were like the cables passing over the piers, and the road they support was like *Diplodocus*'s backbone, which held up the neck and tail.

All about tails

Dinosaur tails had many different uses. Most importantly, the tail helped dinosaurs to move around. Front-heavy dinosaurs used their tails for balance as they walked or ran. Swift flicks of the tail allowed the dinosaur to change direction at speed. Large sauropods probably used their tails as props as they reared to graze on treetop leaves.

Rodlike tail
Deinonychus belonged to a group of birdlike theropods called dromaeosaurids. Its stiffened tail stuck out like a ramrod and helped the feathered theropod to balance as it chased and leapt upon its prey.

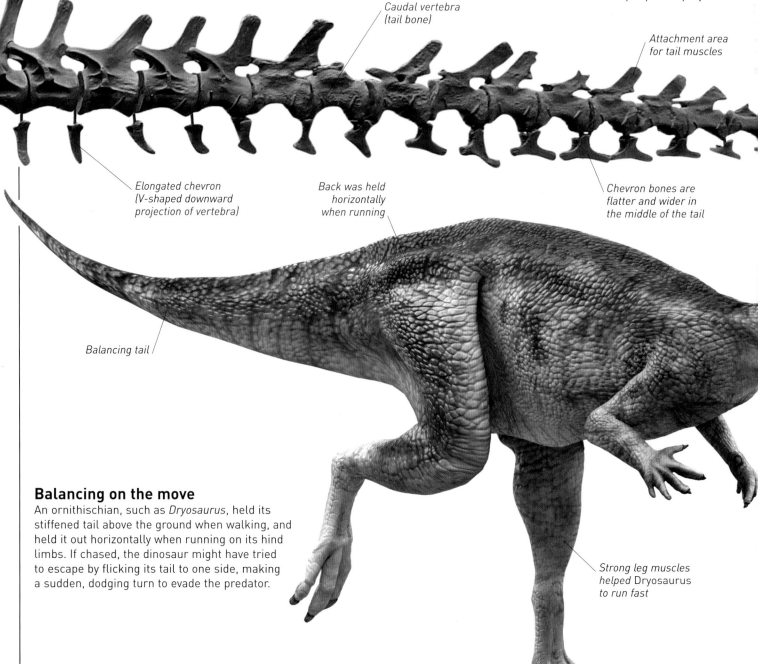

Caudal vertebra (tail bone)

Attachment area for tail muscles

Elongated chevron (V-shaped downward projection of vertebra)

Back was held horizontally when running

Chevron bones are flatter and wider in the middle of the tail

Balancing tail

Balancing on the move
An ornithischian, such as *Dryosaurus*, held its stiffened tail above the ground when walking, and held it out horizontally when running on its hind limbs. If chased, the dinosaur might have tried to escape by flicking its tail to one side, making a sudden, dodging turn to evade the predator.

Strong leg muscles helped Dryosaurus to run fast

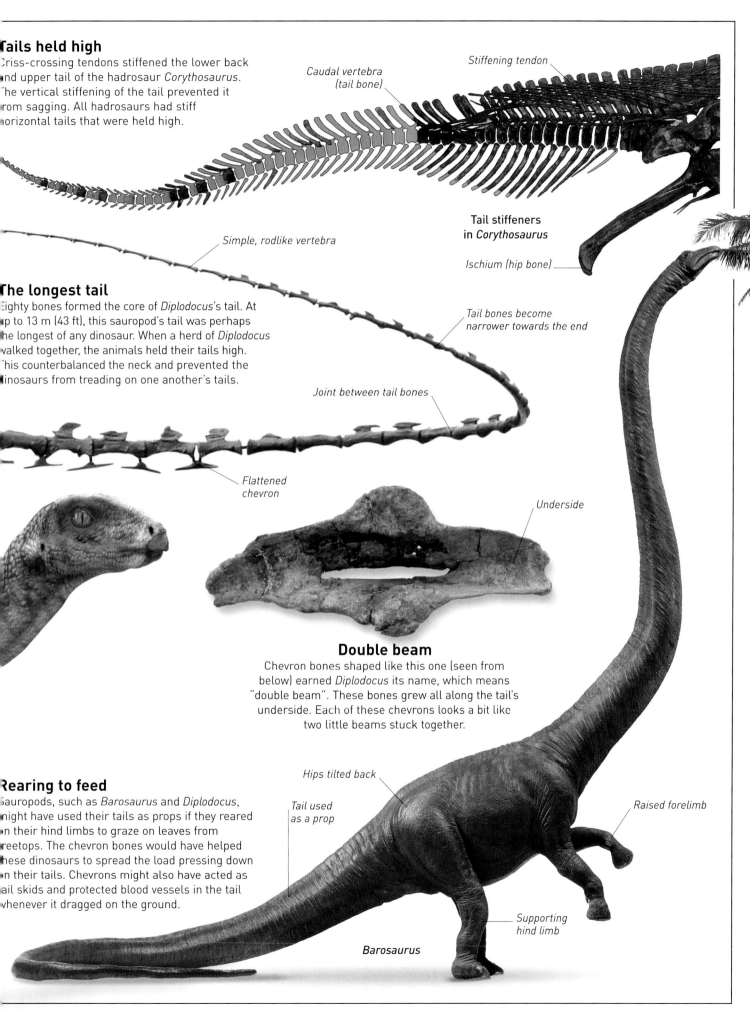

Tails held high

Criss-crossing tendons stiffened the lower back and upper tail of the hadrosaur *Corythosaurus*. The vertical stiffening of the tail prevented it from sagging. All hadrosaurs had stiff horizontal tails that were held high.

Caudal vertebra (tail bone)

Stiffening tendon

Tail stiffeners in *Corythosaurus*

Ischium (hip bone)

The longest tail

Eighty bones formed the core of *Diplodocus*'s tail. At up to 13 m (43 ft), this sauropod's tail was perhaps the longest of any dinosaur. When a herd of *Diplodocus* walked together, the animals held their tails high. This counterbalanced the neck and prevented the dinosaurs from treading on one another's tails.

Simple, rodlike vertebra

Tail bones become narrower towards the end

Joint between tail bones

Flattened chevron

Underside

Double beam

Chevron bones shaped like this one (seen from below) earned *Diplodocus* its name, which means "double beam". These bones grew all along the tail's underside. Each of these chevrons looks a bit like two little beams stuck together.

Rearing to feed

Sauropods, such as *Barosaurus* and *Diplodocus*, might have used their tails as props if they reared on their hind limbs to graze on leaves from treetops. The chevron bones would have helped these dinosaurs to spread the load pressing down on their tails. Chevrons might also have acted as tail skids and protected blood vessels in the tail whenever it dragged on the ground.

Hips tilted back

Tail used as a prop

Raised forelimb

Supporting hind limb

Barosaurus

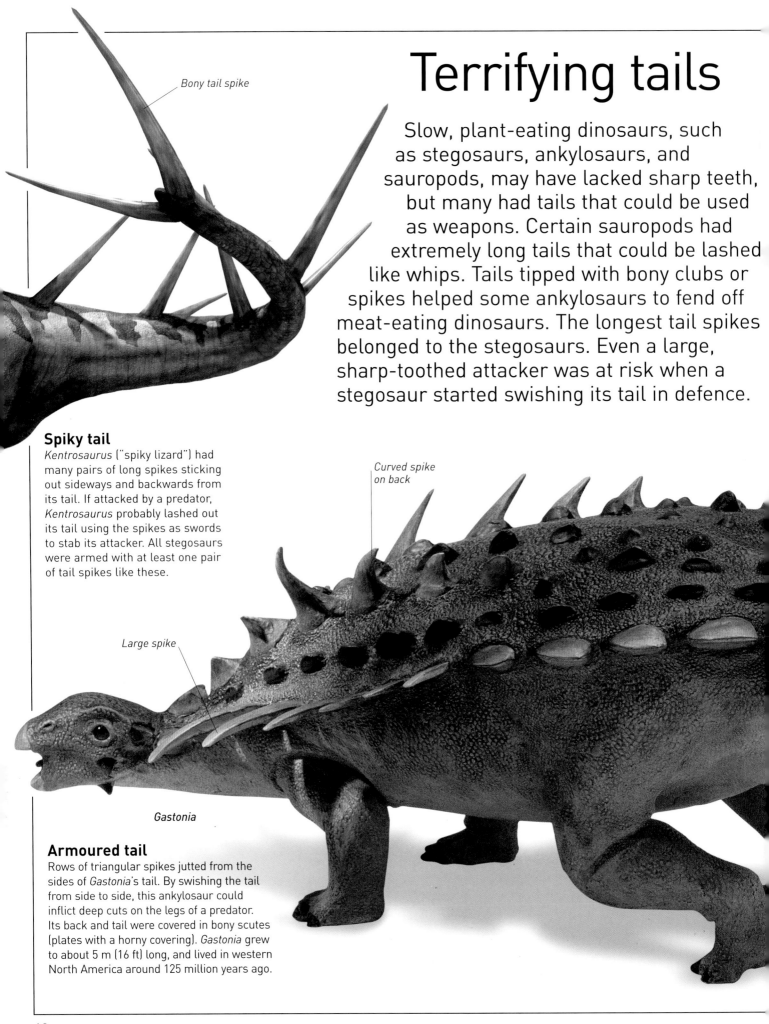

Bony tail spike

Terrifying tails

Slow, plant-eating dinosaurs, such as stegosaurs, ankylosaurs, and sauropods, may have lacked sharp teeth, but many had tails that could be used as weapons. Certain sauropods had extremely long tails that could be lashed like whips. Tails tipped with bony clubs or spikes helped some ankylosaurs to fend off meat-eating dinosaurs. The longest tail spikes belonged to the stegosaurs. Even a large, sharp-toothed attacker was at risk when a stegosaur started swishing its tail in defence.

Spiky tail

Kentrosaurus ("spiky lizard") had many pairs of long spikes sticking out sideways and backwards from its tail. If attacked by a predator, *Kentrosaurus* probably lashed out its tail using the spikes as swords to stab its attacker. All stegosaurs were armed with at least one pair of tail spikes like these.

Curved spike on back

Large spike

Gastonia

Armoured tail

Rows of triangular spikes jutted from the sides of *Gastonia*'s tail. By swishing the tail from side to side, this ankylosaur could inflict deep cuts on the legs of a predator. Its back and tail were covered in bony scutes (plates with a horny covering). *Gastonia* grew to about 5 m (16 ft) long, and lived in western North America around 125 million years ago.

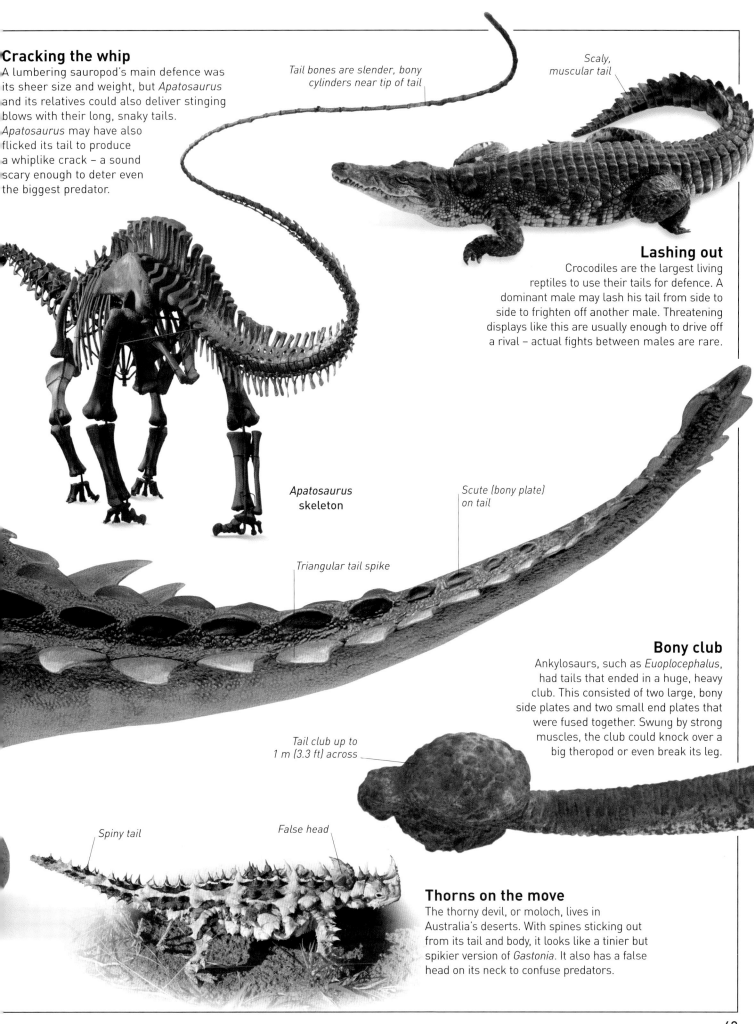

Cracking the whip

A lumbering sauropod's main defence was its sheer size and weight, but *Apatosaurus* and its relatives could also deliver stinging blows with their long, snaky tails. *Apatosaurus* may have also flicked its tail to produce a whiplike crack – a sound scary enough to deter even the biggest predator.

Tail bones are slender, bony cylinders near tip of tail

Scaly, muscular tail

Lashing out

Crocodiles are the largest living reptiles to use their tails for defence. A dominant male may lash his tail from side to side to frighten off another male. Threatening displays like this are usually enough to drive off a rival – actual fights between males are rare.

Apatosaurus skeleton

Scute (bony plate) on tail

Triangular tail spike

Bony club

Ankylosaurs, such as *Euoplocephalus*, had tails that ended in a huge, heavy club. This consisted of two large, bony side plates and two small end plates that were fused together. Swung by strong muscles, the club could knock over a big theropod or even break its leg.

Tail club up to 1 m (3.3 ft) across

Spiny tail

False head

Thorns on the move

The thorny devil, or moloch, lives in Australia's deserts. With spines sticking out from its tail and body, it looks like a tinier but spikier version of *Gastonia*. It also has a false head on its neck to confuse predators.

Plates and sails

In the late Jurassic woodlands, massive *Stegosaurus* with rows of plates on its back must have been quite a sight! Fossils show that features, such as plates, sails, spines, and humps, ran down the backs of many other dinosaurs, including sauropods, ornithopods, and theropods. These structures were covered with horny sheaths, skin, or fatty tissue.

Artery brings hot blood into the plate to lose heat to the cool air

Vein takes cool blood to the bo[...]

Heated debate

Some scientists think that *Stegosaurus*'s plates were covered in skin. The blood vessels under the skin would help to adjust the dinosaur's body temperature. Others believe that the plates were covered in horn, which has no blood vessels, and therefore cannot control temperature.

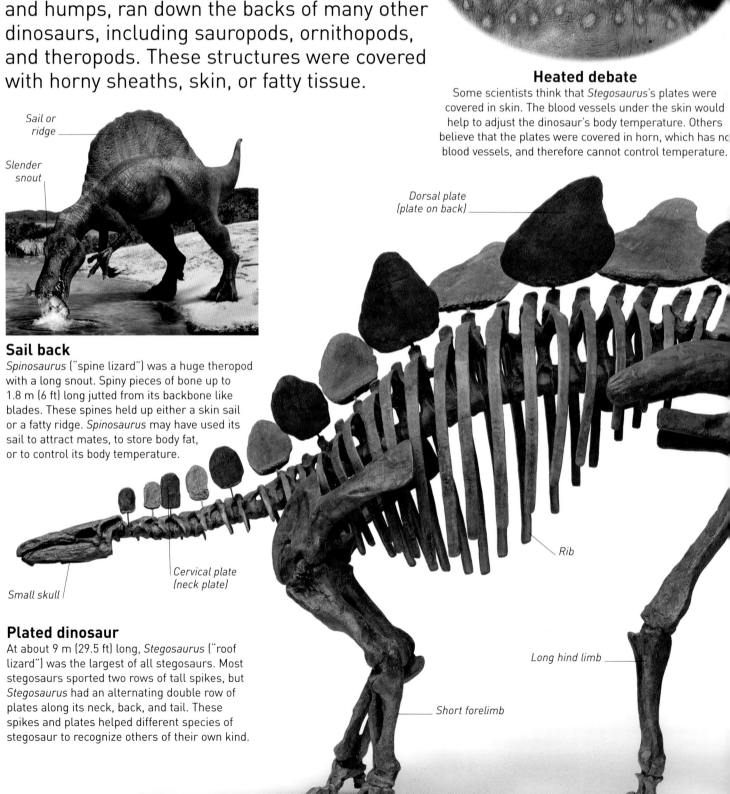

Sail or ridge

Slender snout

Sail back

Spinosaurus ("spine lizard") was a huge theropod with a long snout. Spiny pieces of bone up to 1.8 m (6 ft) long jutted from its backbone like blades. These spines held up either a skin sail or a fatty ridge. *Spinosaurus* may have used its sail to attract mates, to store body fat, or to control its body temperature.

Dorsal plate (plate on back)

Rib

Cervical plate (neck plate)

Small skull

Long hind limb

Short forelimb

Plated dinosaur

At about 9 m (29.5 ft) long, *Stegosaurus* ("roof lizard") was the largest of all stegosaurs. Most stegosaurs sported two rows of tall spikes, but *Stegosaurus* had an alternating double row of plates along its neck, back, and tail. These spikes and plates helped different species of stegosaur to recognize others of their own kind.

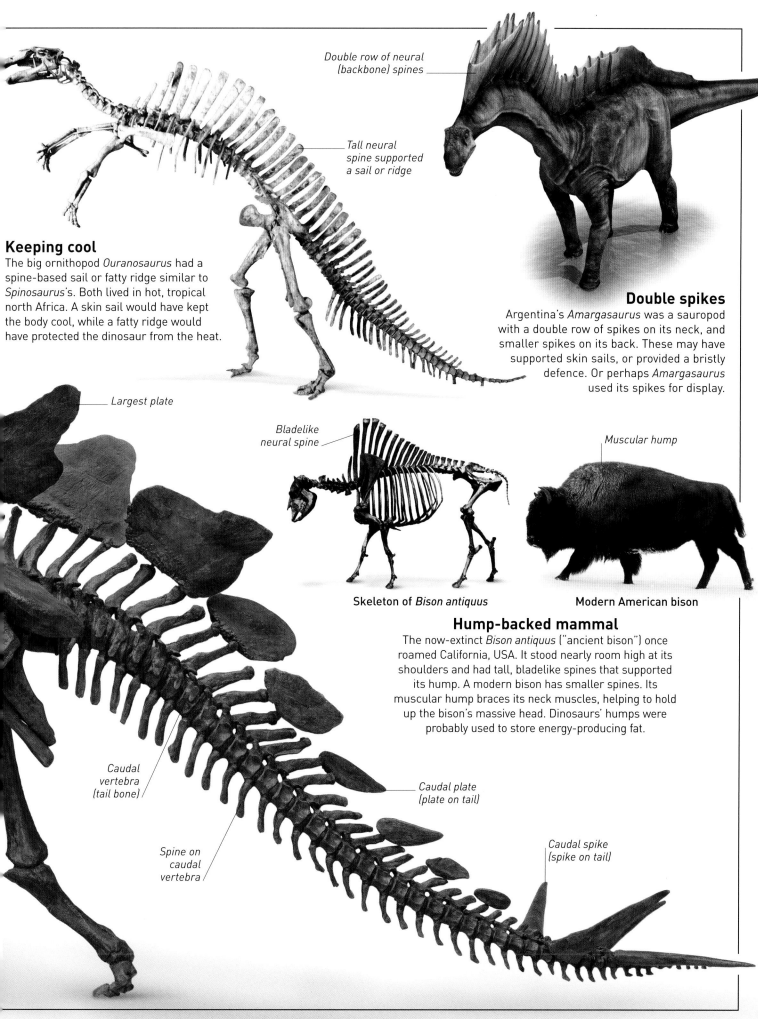

Keeping cool

The big ornithopod *Ouranosaurus* had a spine-based sail or fatty ridge similar to *Spinosaurus*'s. Both lived in hot, tropical north Africa. A skin sail would have kept the body cool, while a fatty ridge would have protected the dinosaur from the heat.

Double row of neural (backbone) spines

Tall neural spine supported a sail or ridge

Double spikes

Argentina's *Amargasaurus* was a sauropod with a double row of spikes on its neck, and smaller spikes on its back. These may have supported skin sails, or provided a bristly defence. Or perhaps *Amargasaurus* used its spikes for display.

Largest plate

Bladelike neural spine

Muscular hump

Skeleton of *Bison antiquus*

Modern American bison

Hump-backed mammal

The now-extinct *Bison antiquus* ("ancient bison") once roamed California, USA. It stood nearly room high at its shoulders and had tall, bladelike spines that supported its hump. A modern bison has smaller spines. Its muscular hump braces its neck muscles, helping to hold up the bison's massive head. Dinosaurs' humps were probably used to store energy-producing fat.

Caudal vertebra (tail bone)

Caudal plate (plate on tail)

Spine on caudal vertebra

Caudal spike (spike on tail)

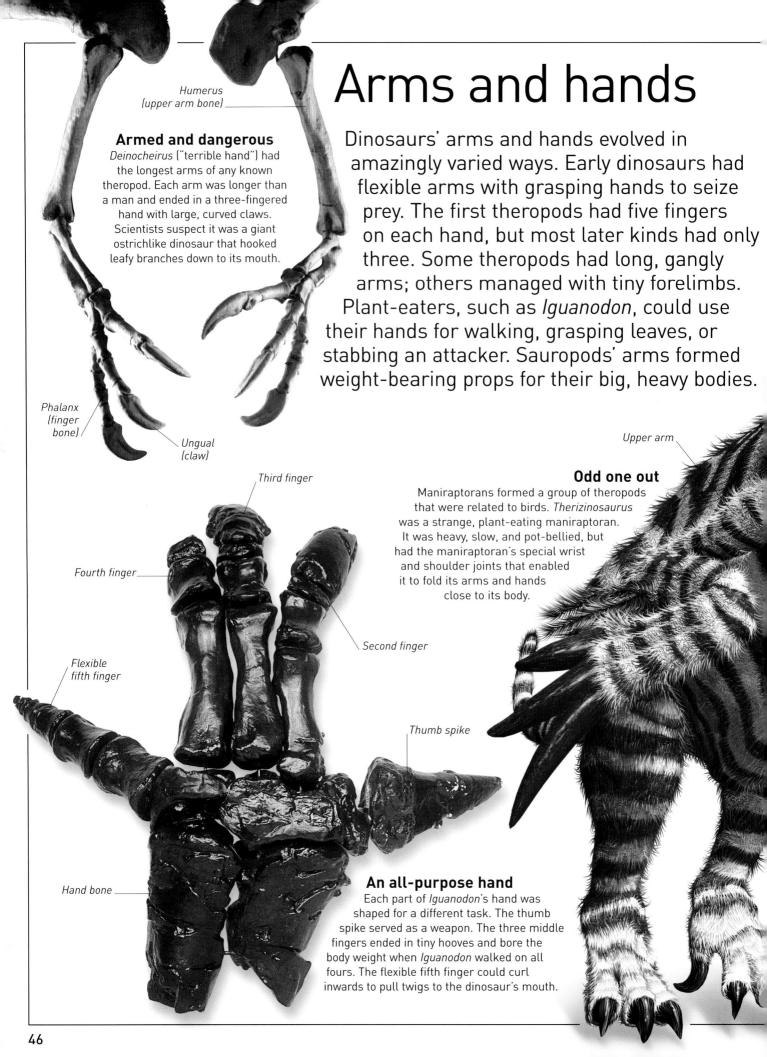

Arms and hands

Dinosaurs' arms and hands evolved in amazingly varied ways. Early dinosaurs had flexible arms with grasping hands to seize prey. The first theropods had five fingers on each hand, but most later kinds had only three. Some theropods had long, gangly arms; others managed with tiny forelimbs. Plant-eaters, such as *Iguanodon*, could use their hands for walking, grasping leaves, or stabbing an attacker. Sauropods' arms formed weight-bearing props for their big, heavy bodies.

Humerus
(upper arm bone)

Armed and dangerous
Deinocheirus ("terrible hand") had the longest arms of any known theropod. Each arm was longer than a man and ended in a three-fingered hand with large, curved claws. Scientists suspect it was a giant ostrichlike dinosaur that hooked leafy branches down to its mouth.

Phalanx
(finger bone)

Ungual
(claw)

Third finger

Fourth finger

Second finger

Flexible fifth finger

Upper arm

Odd one out
Maniraptorans formed a group of theropods that were related to birds. *Therizinosaurus* was a strange, plant-eating maniraptoran. It was heavy, slow, and pot-bellied, but had the maniraptoran's special wrist and shoulder joints that enabled it to fold its arms and hands close to its body.

Thumb spike

Hand bone

An all-purpose hand
Each part of *Iguanodon*'s hand was shaped for a different task. The thumb spike served as a weapon. The three middle fingers ended in tiny hooves and bore the body weight when *Iguanodon* walked on all fours. The flexible fifth finger could curl inwards to pull twigs to the dinosaur's mouth.

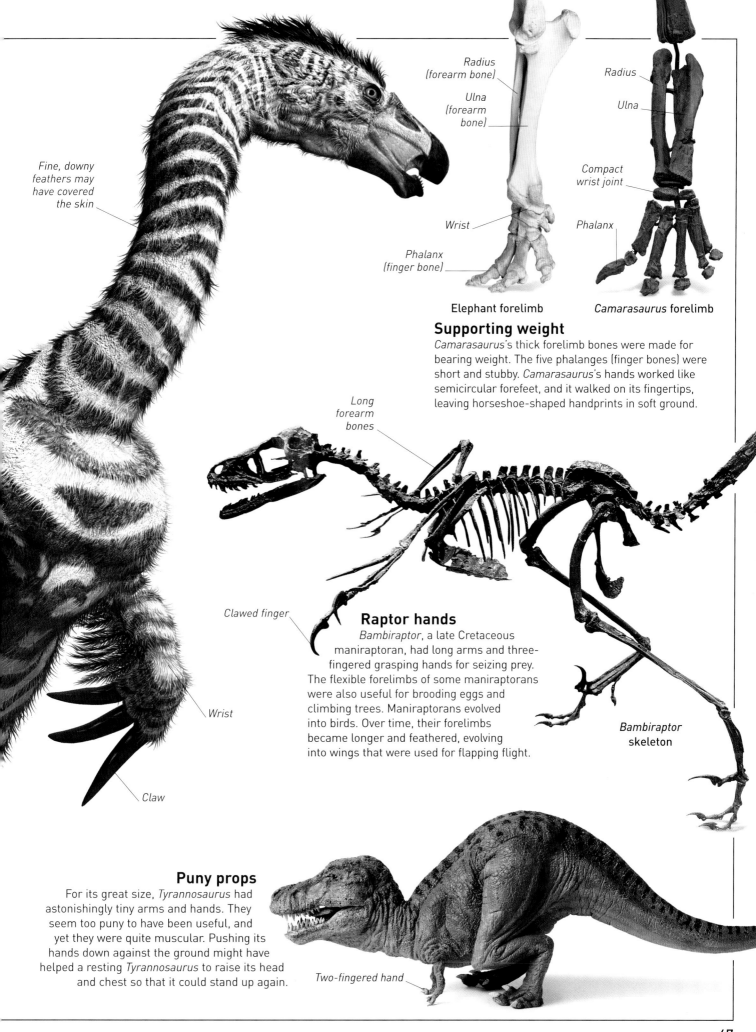

Fine, downy feathers may have covered the skin

Radius (forearm bone)

Ulna (forearm bone)

Radius

Ulna

Compact wrist joint

Wrist

Phalanx (finger bone)

Phalanx

Elephant forelimb

***Camarasaurus* forelimb**

Supporting weight

Camarasaurus's thick forelimb bones were made for bearing weight. The five phalanges (finger bones) were short and stubby. *Camarasaurus*'s hands worked like semicircular forefeet, and it walked on its fingertips, leaving horseshoe-shaped handprints in soft ground.

Long forearm bones

Clawed finger

Raptor hands

Bambiraptor, a late Cretaceous maniraptoran, had long arms and three-fingered grasping hands for seizing prey. The flexible forelimbs of some maniraptorans were also useful for brooding eggs and climbing trees. Maniraptorans evolved into birds. Over time, their forelimbs became longer and feathered, evolving into wings that were used for flapping flight.

Wrist

Claw

Bambiraptor skeleton

Puny props

For its great size, *Tyrannosaurus* had astonishingly tiny arms and hands. They seem too puny to have been useful, and yet they were quite muscular. Pushing its hands down against the ground might have helped a resting *Tyrannosaurus* to raise its head and chest so that it could stand up again.

Two-fingered hand

Claws and their uses

Claws can tell us much about how dinosaurs lived. Predatory dinosaurs used sharp, curved claws on their narrow fingers as weapons. A group of maniraptorans called dromaeosaurids often tackled plant-eaters larger than themselves with their big, sharp toe claws. But the longest claws of all belonged to the strange plant-eating theropod, *Therizinosaurus*. Most plant-eaters had claws that had evolved into short, stubby nails or small hooves to protect the fingers and toes from wear. Some ornithischians may have used their claws for digging up plants or burrowing.

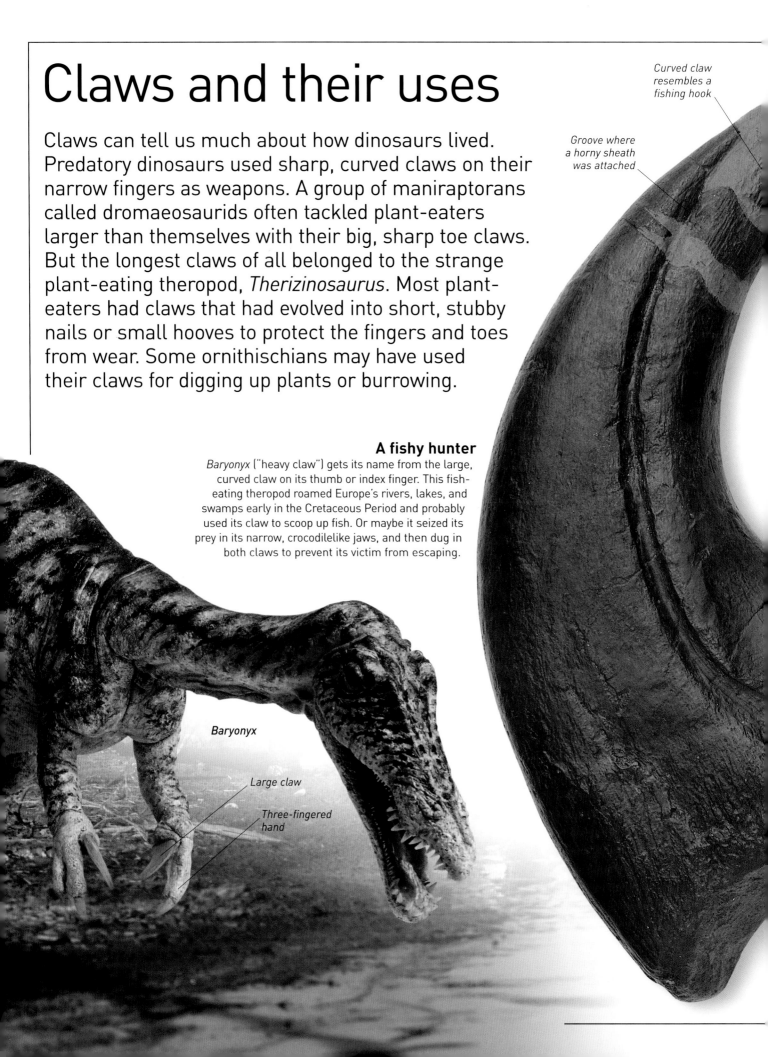

Curved claw resembles a fishing hook

Groove where a horny sheath was attached

A fishy hunter
Baryonyx ("heavy claw") gets its name from the large, curved claw on its thumb or index finger. This fish-eating theropod roamed Europe's rivers, lakes, and swamps early in the Cretaceous Period and probably used its claw to scoop up fish. Or maybe it seized its prey in its narrow, crocodilelike jaws, and then dug in both claws to prevent its victim from escaping.

Baryonyx

Large claw

Three-fingered hand

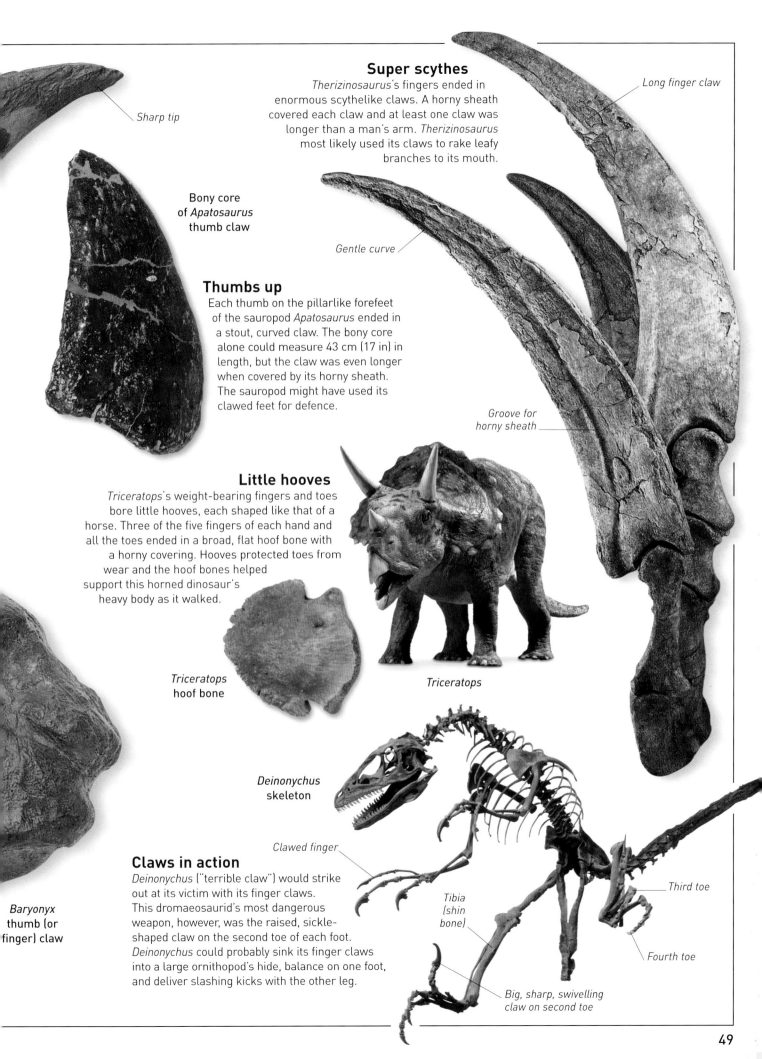

Sharp tip

Super scythes

Therizinosaurus's fingers ended in enormous scythelike claws. A horny sheath covered each claw and at least one claw was longer than a man's arm. *Therizinosaurus* most likely used its claws to rake leafy branches to its mouth.

Long finger claw

Bony core of *Apatosaurus* thumb claw

Gentle curve

Thumbs up

Each thumb on the pillarlike forefeet of the sauropod *Apatosaurus* ended in a stout, curved claw. The bony core alone could measure 43 cm (17 in) in length, but the claw was even longer when covered by its horny sheath. The sauropod might have used its clawed feet for defence.

Groove for horny sheath

Little hooves

Triceratops's weight-bearing fingers and toes bore little hooves, each shaped like that of a horse. Three of the five fingers of each hand and all the toes ended in a broad, flat hoof bone with a horny covering. Hooves protected toes from wear and the hoof bones helped support this horned dinosaur's heavy body as it walked.

Triceratops hoof bone

Triceratops

Deinonychus skeleton

Clawed finger

Claws in action

Deinonychus ("terrible claw") would strike out at its victim with its finger claws. This dromaeosaurid's most dangerous weapon, however, was the raised, sickle-shaped claw on the second toe of each foot. *Deinonychus* could probably sink its finger claws into a large ornithopod's hide, balance on one foot, and deliver slashing kicks with the other leg.

Baryonyx thumb (or finger) claw

Tibia (shin bone)

Third toe

Fourth toe

Big, sharp, swivelling claw on second toe

Legs and feet

Fast-moving dinosaurs, such as theropods, walked and ran only on their hind limbs. The quickest dinosaurs had slim legs with long shins, and narrow feet with birdlike toes. In contrast, the heavy, plodding sauropods had thick, weight-bearing legs and short, broad feet. All dinosaurs walked on their toes and had vertical legs. The thigh bones fitted into the side of the hip bones through a ball-and-socket joint, similar to those in our hips.

Femur
(thigh bone)

Tibia
(shin bone)

Fibula
(calf bone)

Metatarsal (foot bone)

Hypsilophodon hind limb

Toe

Built for speed

Hypsilophodon's long leg bones – made up of the shin, calf, foot, and toe bones – show that this timid plant-eater could run fast. If it lived today, *Hypsilophodon* would stand no more than waist-high to a man, yet this small ornithopod could probably outrun an athlete.

Allosaurus

Long, curved neck

Three-fingered hand on short forelimb

Long, bony tail

Ornithomimus

The great escape

Ornithomimus ("bird mimic") was a long-legged dinosaur that resembled an ostrich, except for its arms and tail. Speed was its only defence and, like ostriches, a herd of ornithomimids could sprint from danger at up to 64 kph (40 mph).

Ankle joint

Long metatarsal (foot bone)

Phalanx (toe bone)

Ostriches in the Etosha salt pan, Namibia

Plodding giant

Large sauropods, such as *Vulcanodon*, trudged along very slowly. Their solid leg bones had evolved not for running, but to support a huge, heavy body. Most sauropods were large enough to ignore most theropod predators.

Vulcanodon

Pillarlike limb

Tibia

High ankle joint

Long metatarsal

Phalanx

Hallux

Theropod's foot

Theropods ("beast feet") get their name from their sharp, curved claws. A typical theropod foot, like this *Tyrannosaurus* foot, had three main toes, and a little hallux (big toe) that had evolved into a spike at the back of the foot.

Massive tibia

Low ankle joint

Short metatarsal

Phalanx

Sauropod's foot

Diplodocus's hind limbs were thick and strong to carry its weight. Each of the pillarlike legs rested on a broad, five-toed foot. The legs and feet of a sauropod resembled those of a modern elephant.

Powerful thigh

On the run

Some scientists think that *Allosaurus*'s powerful legs drove this predator along at speeds of up to 32 kph (20 mph) when it was chasing prey. But a large and short-armed theropod, such as an *Allosaurus*, risked serious injury if it fell while running fast. Many scientists do not believe that this theropod could run faster than a human jogger.

High ankle

Weight-bearing toes

Ancient footprints

Dinosaurs sometimes left their footprints in soft mud, which quickly dried and hardened. The footprints became buried in layers of mud, which turned into rock, preserving the footprints as fossils. The shapes and sizes of such prints and the gaps between them can help scientists to identify which dinosaurs made the prints. They can also work out the sizes of the dinosaurs and how fast they moved.

Thunder foot
Fossil sauropod footprints found in rocks in Purgatoire in Colorado, USA, tell us that a herd of diplodocid dinosaurs passed by some time late in the Jurassic Period. Scientists were not sure exactly which dinosaur made the gigantic Purgatoire prints, so they gave it a special name – *Brontopodus*, meaning "thunder foot".

Inner toe print

Ilium (hip bone)

Hip height

Iguanodon **skeleton**

Length of foot

Calculating size
Scientists can estimate the size of a dinosaur, such as this *Iguanodon*, from just its footprints without even seeing its fossil bones. Multiplying the size of a footprint by four gives an idea of the dinosaur's hip height. Scientists can then work out the likely length of the whole animal.

Fossil tracks
Scientists have identified 150,000 fossil tracks in a square patch of land, 1 km (0.6 miles) across, in Wyoming, USA. Tracing individual dinosaur footprints can be difficult. As shown here, the survival of only the hindfeet prints of a four-legged dinosaur might wrongly suggest that they came from a two-legged dinosaur.

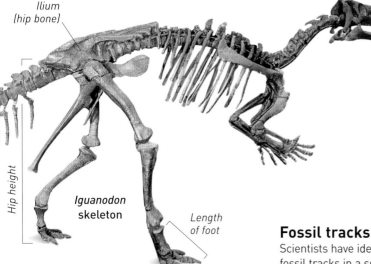

Small dinosaur's hindfeet leave lighter impressions on mud

Wet surface

Mudflat

Large dinosaur hindfoot make deep impressio[n]

1 Making footprints
A small two-legged dinosaur and a large four-legged dinosaur both leave footprints on the surface mud, but only the large dinosaur's hindfeet make dents in the firm lower layer.

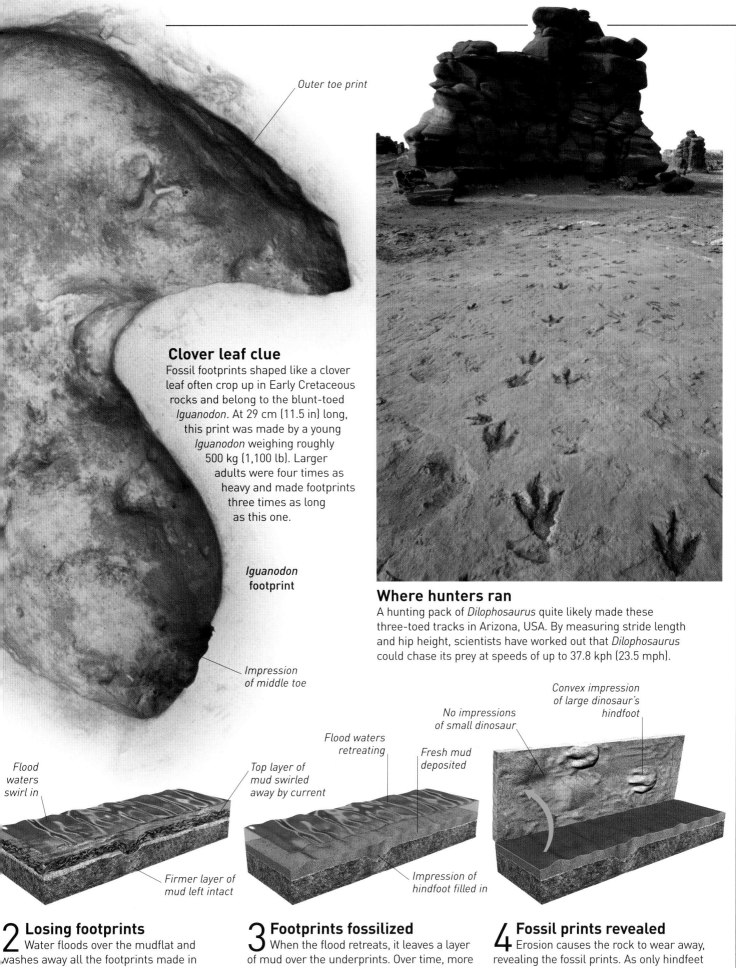

Outer toe print

Clover leaf clue

Fossil footprints shaped like a clover leaf often crop up in Early Cretaceous rocks and belong to the blunt-toed *Iguanodon*. At 29 cm (11.5 in) long, this print was made by a young *Iguanodon* weighing roughly 500 kg (1,100 lb). Larger adults were four times as heavy and made footprints three times as long as this one.

Iguanodon **footprint**

Impression of middle toe

Where hunters ran

A hunting pack of *Dilophosaurus* quite likely made these three-toed tracks in Arizona, USA. By measuring stride length and hip height, scientists have worked out that *Dilophosaurus* could chase its prey at speeds of up to 37.8 kph (23.5 mph).

Convex impression of large dinosaur's hindfoot

No impressions of small dinosaur

Flood waters retreating

Fresh mud deposited

Flood waters swirl in

Top layer of mud swirled away by current

Firmer layer of mud left intact

Impression of hindfoot filled in

2 Losing footprints

Water floods over the mudflat and washes away all the footprints made in the soft surface mud. Only the underprints formed in the lower layer survive.

3 Footprints fossilized

When the flood retreats, it leaves a layer of mud over the underprints. Over time, more floods dump mud in layers that harden into rock. Inside, the underprints survive as fossils.

4 Fossil prints revealed

Erosion causes the rock to wear away, revealing the fossil prints. As only hindfeet prints survive, it is easy to assume that a two-legged dinosaur had made them.

Tough skins

A typical dinosaur's skin was waterproof and scaly, similar to that of a lizard or crocodile. It protected the dinosaur's body from shrivelling up in hot, dry conditions. The skin was also tough, so it was not easily cut in a fall or fight. Some dinosaurs had skins with bony armour for extra protection. Quite likely, big dinosaurs had drab colours like elephants, but small dinosaurs might have had bright colours for display or camouflage.

Bright pattern on skin

Reptilian skin
The Gila monster's skin is covered in bumpy scales arranged like tiny pebbles. From skin impressions preserved in rocks, we know that dinosaurs had scales like this.

Pea-sized ossicles (bony lumps)

Saltasaurus

Armoured hide

Coat of armour
The backs and sides of *Saltasaurus*, and some other dinosaurs in a group of sauropods called titanosaurs, were strengthened with layers of flexible armour. Set into their hides were thousands of bony lumps ranging in size from peas to dinner plates.

Saltasaurus skin impression

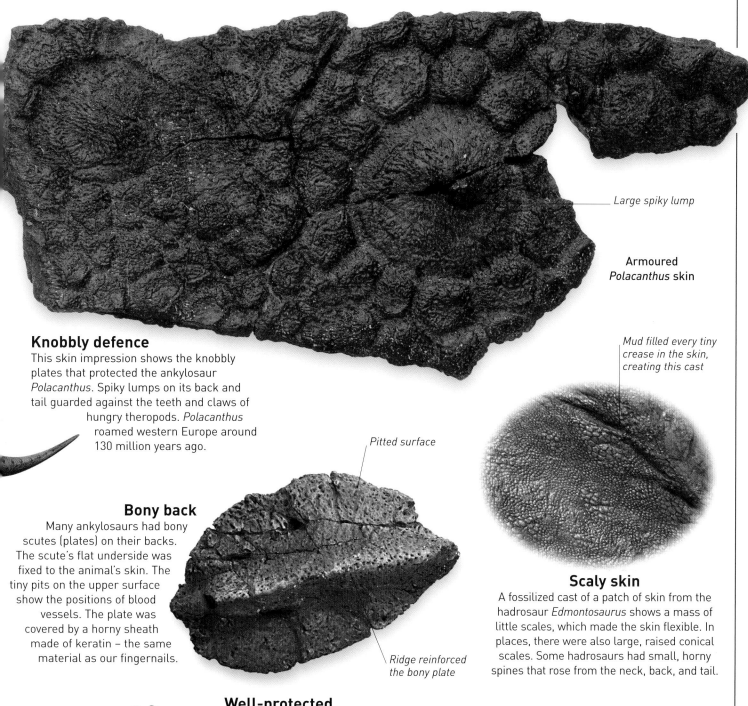

Large spiky lump

Armoured
Polacanthus skin

Knobbly defence

This skin impression shows the knobbly plates that protected the ankylosaur *Polacanthus*. Spiky lumps on its back and tail guarded against the teeth and claws of hungry theropods. *Polacanthus* roamed western Europe around 130 million years ago.

Mud filled every tiny crease in the skin, creating this cast

Pitted surface

Bony back

Many ankylosaurs had bony scutes (plates) on their backs. The scute's flat underside was fixed to the animal's skin. The tiny pits on the upper surface show the positions of blood vessels. The plate was covered by a horny sheath made of keratin – the same material as our fingernails.

Ridge reinforced the bony plate

Scaly skin

A fossilized cast of a patch of skin from the hadrosaur *Edmontosaurus* shows a mass of little scales, which made the skin flexible. In places, there were also large, raised conical scales. Some hadrosaurs had small, horny spines that rose from the neck, back, and tail.

Well-protected

The ankylosaur *Edmontonia* bristled with armour. It had bony plates on its skull, neck, and shoulders, and spikes on its shoulders and sides. Small, ridged plates covered the back, hips, and tail.

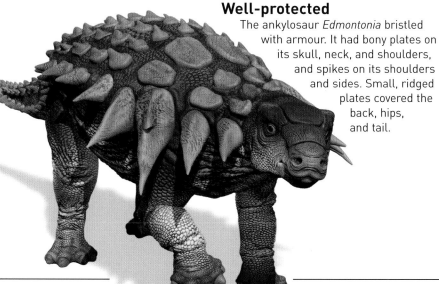

Armoured armadillo

Some modern mammals, such as armadillos, have similar defences to those of the ankylosaurs. Bands of scutes (plates) run across an armadillo's body, and stiff shields guard the hips and shoulders. The weakest spot is the unprotected belly.

Feathers

Not all dinosaurs had scaly skin – some were covered in down or feathers. Discovered in Germany in 1861, *Archaeopteryx* was a primitive bird with wings, clawed fingers, and a long, bony tail. In 1996, scientists discovered *Sinosauropteryx,* a small, birdlike dinosaur with a downy covering on its body. The first featherlike structures might have been used for keeping the body warm. Feathers used for display and flight probably developed later.

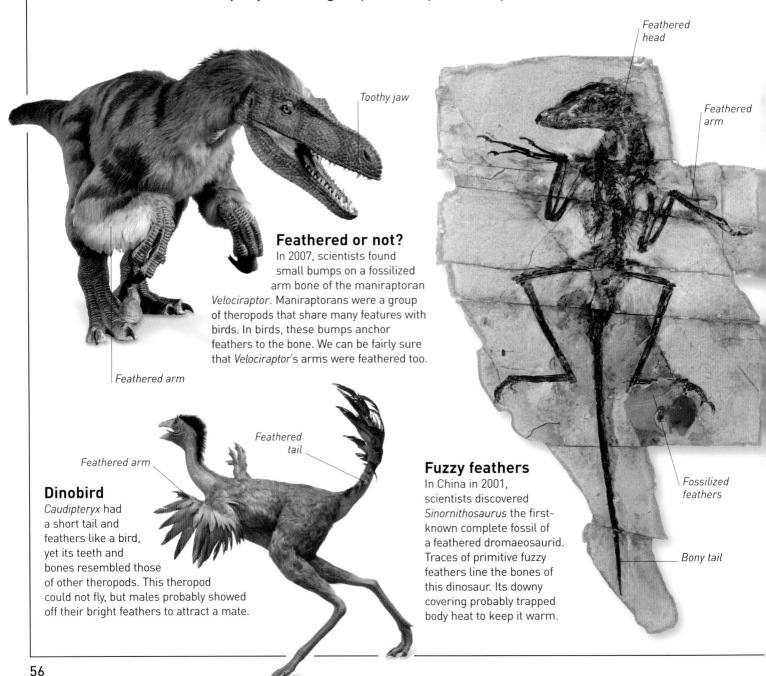

Toothy jaw

Feathered head

Feathered arm

Feathered or not?
In 2007, scientists found small bumps on a fossilized arm bone of the maniraptoran *Velociraptor*. Maniraptorans were a group of theropods that share many features with birds. In birds, these bumps anchor feathers to the bone. We can be fairly sure that *Velociraptor*'s arms were feathered too.

Feathered arm

Feathered tail

Feathered arm

Dinobird
Caudipteryx had a short tail and feathers like a bird, yet its teeth and bones resembled those of other theropods. This theropod could not fly, but males probably showed off their bright feathers to attract a mate.

Fuzzy feathers
In China in 2001, scientists discovered *Sinornithosaurus* the first-known complete fossil of a feathered dromaeosaurid. Traces of primitive fuzzy feathers line the bones of this dinosaur. Its downy covering probably trapped body heat to keep it warm.

Fossilized feathers

Bony tail

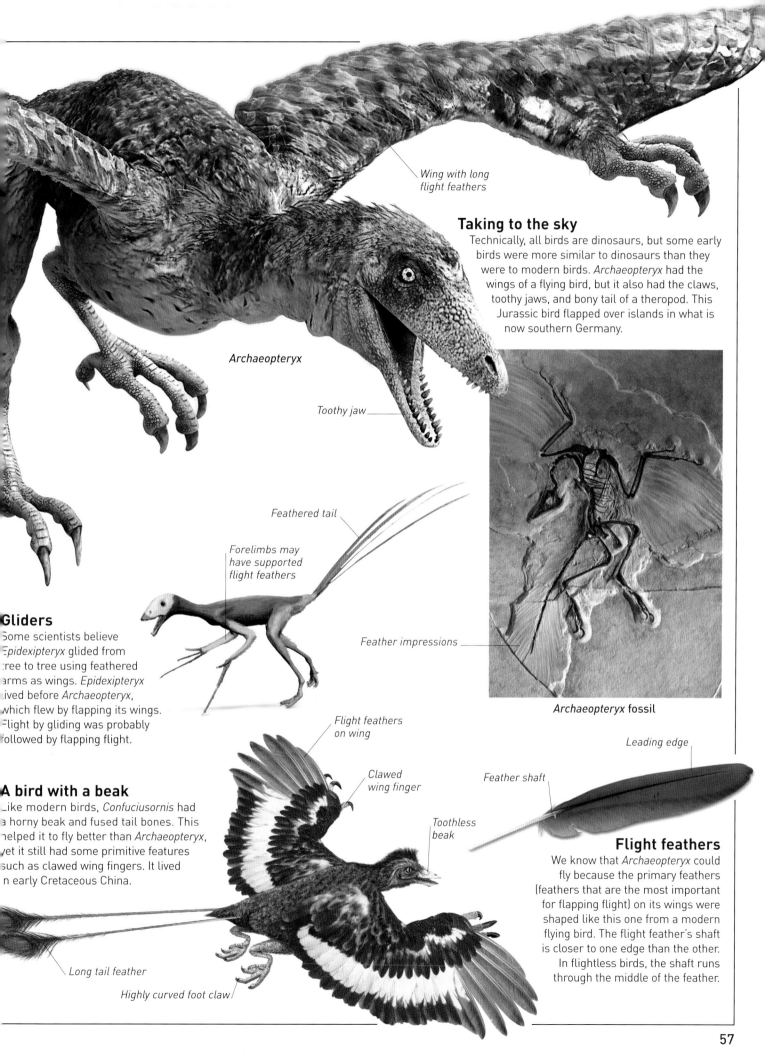

Wing with long flight feathers

Archaeopteryx

Toothy jaw

Taking to the sky
Technically, all birds are dinosaurs, but some early birds were more similar to dinosaurs than they were to modern birds. *Archaeopteryx* had the wings of a flying bird, but it also had the claws, toothy jaws, and bony tail of a theropod. This Jurassic bird flapped over islands in what is now southern Germany.

Feathered tail

Forelimbs may have supported flight feathers

Feather impressions

Archaeopteryx fossil

Gliders
Some scientists believe *Epidexipteryx* glided from tree to tree using feathered arms as wings. *Epidexipteryx* lived before *Archaeopteryx*, which flew by flapping its wings. Flight by gliding was probably followed by flapping flight.

Flight feathers on wing

Clawed wing finger

Toothless beak

Leading edge

Feather shaft

A bird with a beak
Like modern birds, *Confuciusornis* had a horny beak and fused tail bones. This helped it to fly better than *Archaeopteryx*, yet it still had some primitive features such as clawed wing fingers. It lived in early Cretaceous China.

Long tail feather

Highly curved foot claw

Flight feathers
We know that *Archaeopteryx* could fly because the primary feathers (feathers that are the most important for flapping flight) on its wings were shaped like this one from a modern flying bird. The flight feather's shaft is closer to one edge than the other. In flightless birds, the shaft runs through the middle of the feather.

Eggs and young

Dinosaurs hatched from hard-shelled eggs like those of birds and crocodiles. By studying a fossil eggshell's shape and texture, palaeontologists can tell which type of dinosaur laid the egg. Sometimes they even find a tiny skeleton inside the fossil egg. Small dinosaurs probably sat on their eggs to warm them, but big dinosaurs hatched their eggs with warmth from sunshine or rotting vegetation. Some dinosaurs ran around and started looking for food soon after hatching. Others needed parental care until they could fend for themselves.

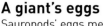

A giant's eggs

Sauropods' eggs measured about 13 cm (5 in) across and were protected by a thick shell. These eggs seem small for the size of the huge dinosaurs that laid them, but larger eggs would have needed shells so thick that hatchlings could not have broken out.

Damage caused during fossilization

Head tucked in

Ready to hatch

Tiny bones found in a fossil egg helped a model-maker to create this lifelike restoration of a *Troodon* about to hatch. Such eggs have been found at Egg Mountain, a late Cretaceous fossil site in Montana, USA. *Troodon* mothers laid eggs two at a time. Their hatchlings ran around quickly after birth to look for food.

Tail tucked under body

Elongated shape

Stolen goods?

Oviraptor, and its relatives the oviraptorids, laid narrow, hard-shelled eggs. *Oviraptor* means "egg thief". Scientists once thought that *Oviraptor* used to steal eggs laid by plant-eater *Protoceratops*. They realized their mistake when they found fossils of an oviraptorid sitting on similar eggs to these.

Dino kids

This model shows *Maiasaura* hatchlings crouching in the protection of their mud-mound nest among unhatched eggs. *Maiasaura* was a large hadrosaur and dozens of individuals nested close together. The mothers fed their babies in the nests until they were strong enough to leave.

Growing up

From left to right, *Protoceratops* fossils show how this plant-eater's skull changed as it grew up. The beak became tall and narrow, the bony frill at the back of the skull grew bigger, and the cheeks flared out at the sides.

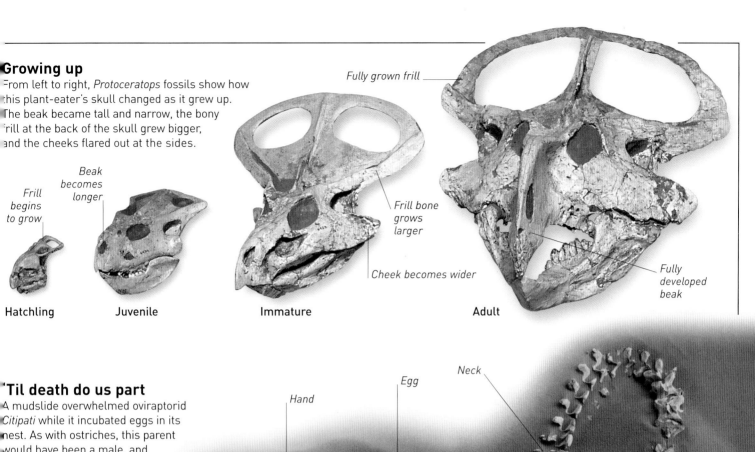

Frill begins to grow

Beak becomes longer

Fully grown frill

Frill bone grows larger

Cheek becomes wider

Fully developed beak

Hatchling

Juvenile

Immature

Adult

"Til death do us part

A mudslide overwhelmed oviraptorid *Citipati* while it incubated eggs in its nest. As with ostriches, this parent would have been a male, and several females might have laid the eggs in its care. This particular *Citipati* died with its feathered arms spread out to shield the eggs from the weather. *Citipati* lived in what is now Mongolia's Gobi Desert.

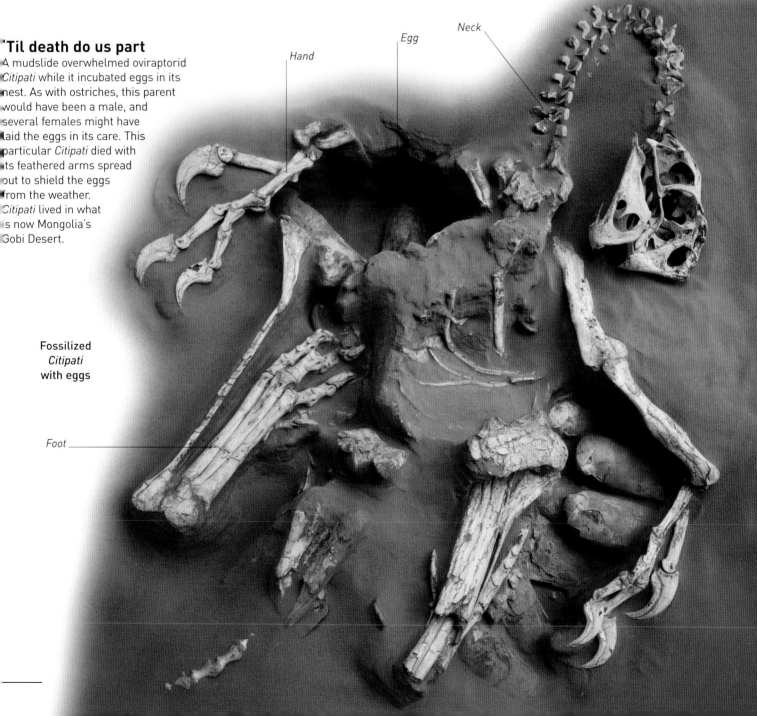

Hand

Egg

Neck

Fossilized *Citipati* with eggs

Foot

Finding fossils

Fossil hunters looking for dinosaur bones must first identify the right kinds of rocks. Dinosaur fossils are usually found buried in sedimentary rocks like sandstones, in barren deserts, cliffs, and quarries. Discovering the bones is just the start. Experts may work for weeks to excavate a large fossil without damaging it. Meanwhile, they measure, map, and photograph each bone.

Ancient treasure trove
This palaeontologist is excavating a sauropodomorph skeleton in China's Lufeng Basin. In 1938, palaeontologist Yang Zhongjian unearthed fossils of the prosauropod *Lufengosaurus*. Since then, the area has yielded more than 100 dinosaur skeletons from the Jurassic Period.

The hunt
In the Dinosaur Provincial Park in Alberta, Canada, palaeontologist Hans Larsson perches precariously halfway up a cliff to excavate a toe bone of *Centrosaurus*, a horned dinosaur.

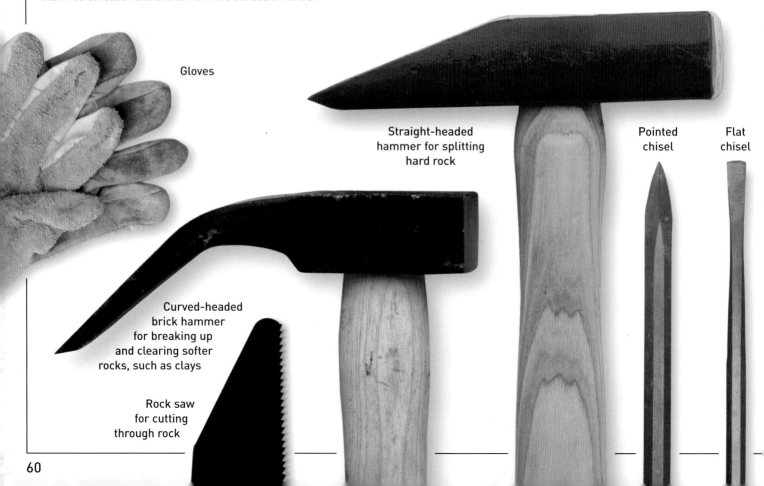

Gloves

Straight-headed hammer for splitting hard rock

Pointed chisel

Flat chisel

Curved-headed brick hammer for breaking up and clearing softer rocks, such as clays

Rock saw for cutting through rock

The find

When excavating dinosaur bones, palaeontologists use hammers and chisels to clear away the rocky material surrounding the bones. Next, they wrap the bones in sackcloth soaked in wet plaster. This sets quickly, forming a strong, rigid coat. Each plaster jacket protects the fragile fossil bone inside against damage on the ride to the laboratory.

1 Cleaning a limb bone
The palaeontologists carefully brush away dirt from the fossil bone before encasing it in plaster.

2 Making a plaster cast
Then they apply runny plaster of Paris to sackcloth bandages and wrap these around the bone.

3 Preparing for study
When the bone arrives at the laboratory, technicians remove the cast so the bone can be studied.

Tools of the trade

Palaeontologists use tools like these to free fossils from rock, to clean them, and to pack them safely. They might paint fragile bones with watery glue to stop them from crumbling, and then encase the bones in a plaster jacket. Or they might wrap the bones in aluminium foil and then pour on chemicals producing polyurethane foam, which expands and covers the fossils to protect them.

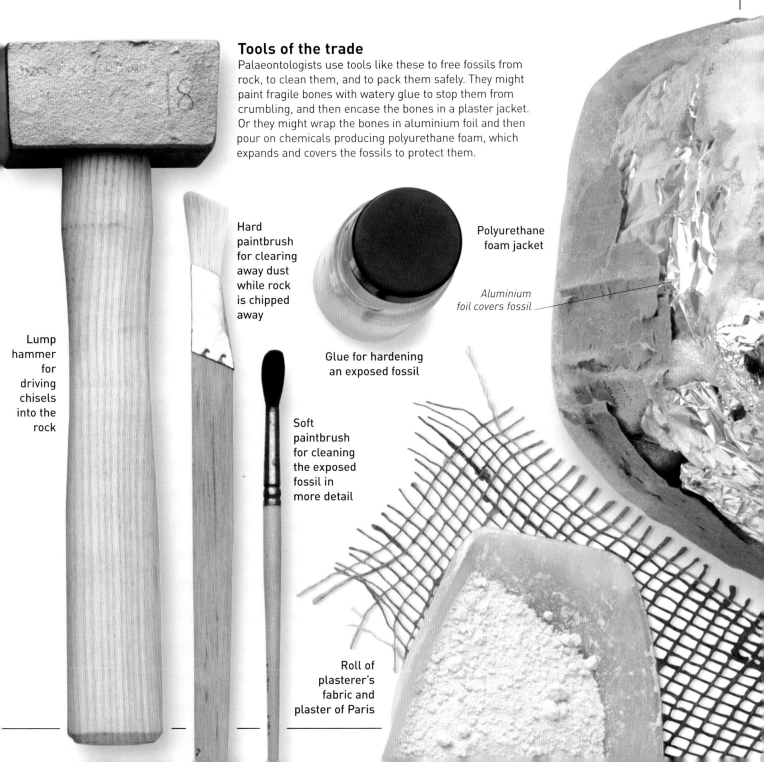

Lump hammer for driving chisels into the rock

Hard paintbrush for clearing away dust while rock is chipped away

Glue for hardening an exposed fossil

Soft paintbrush for cleaning the exposed fossil in more detail

Polyurethane foam jacket

Aluminium foil covers fossil

Roll of plasterer's fabric and plaster of Paris

Rebuilding a dinosaur

Digging up a dinosaur's bones is just the first step in learning what it looked like. In the museum laboratory, technicians saw off the plaster coats protecting the bones and chip away any hard rock with chisels. They use tools like dentists' drills for detailed work, and may even use acid on certain kinds of stone. Once the bones are cleaned, palaeontologists can reconstruct the dinosaur's skeleton by fitting them together. Model-makers can then build a lifelike restoration of the animal.

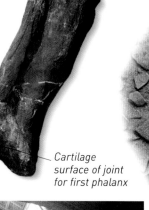

Exposing the fossil
A technician uses acid to reveal embryos hidden in fossil dinosaur eggs. Each day, acid eats away a wafer-thin layer of the stony material around the embryos. This process can take up to a year.

Cartilage cap of ankle joint

Finding clues
Fossil bones can tell us about muscles and other tissues that have vanished. The upper end of this *Iguanodon* foot bone shows where cartilage (gristle) protected the ankle joint. The bottom end is where cartilage protected the bone against the first toe bone (phalanx).

Cartilage surface of joint for first phalanx

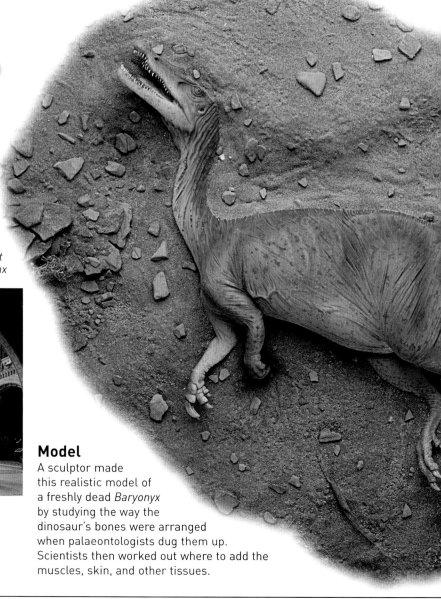

On display
A cast of a *Diplodocus* skeleton stands in the main hall of London's Natural History Museum. Museums worldwide display replicas of dinosaur skeletons. The replicas are cast from moulds made from real fossils.

Model
A sculptor made this realistic model of a freshly dead *Baryonyx* by studying the way the dinosaur's bones were arranged when palaeontologists dug them up. Scientists then worked out where to add the muscles, skin, and other tissues.

Digital dinosaurs

Special 3-D modelling and computer software allow graphic artists to create digital models of dinosaurs, such as this *Corythosaurus*. They first draw a body framework in the software. Then they add details, such as colour and texture to the skin.

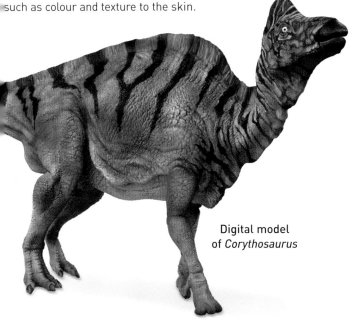

Digital model
of *Corythosaurus*

Reconstruction
of lake bed

Baryonyx
restoration

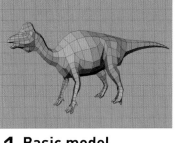

1 Basic model
The first step is to study the dinosaur's bones and make a basic model from geometric shapes on a computer.

2 Shaping the dinosaur
Software divides the shapes into millions of smaller units. An artist can then sculpt these units to refine the dinosaur's shape.

3 Making it accurate
New discoveries about a dinosaur, such as the size and shape of its crest, are added to the model to make it accurate.

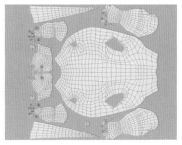

4 UV mapping
3-D painting tools add basic colour to the model. A technique called UV mapping helps to add further colour and texture.

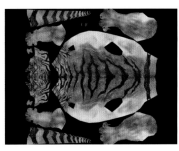

5 Adding colour
The artist creates detailed colour maps of the skin that consist of tints, shades, and tones of different colours.

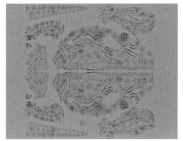

6 Adding more detail
UV mapping can also make one part of a dinosaur's body appear to be glossier or scalier than another.

7 Rigging
A rigger (a programmer who is an expert in anatomy) tells the computer how different parts of the body would have moved.

8 Putting it together
The colours and texture are now applied to the model. The dinosaur is then placed against a realistic background.

Classifying dinosaurs

Each kind of dinosaur is called a species, and one or more related species make up a genus. A species together with all of its descendants forms a group called a clade. This diagram (cladogram) shows how most of the main groups of dinosaur were related.

Pioneers of classification

In 1735, Sweden's Carl Linnaeus classified living things into species. In 1887, Britain's Harry Govier Seeley (above) classified dinosaurs as ornithischians and saurischians. In 1950, German's Willi Hennig began to group species into clades.

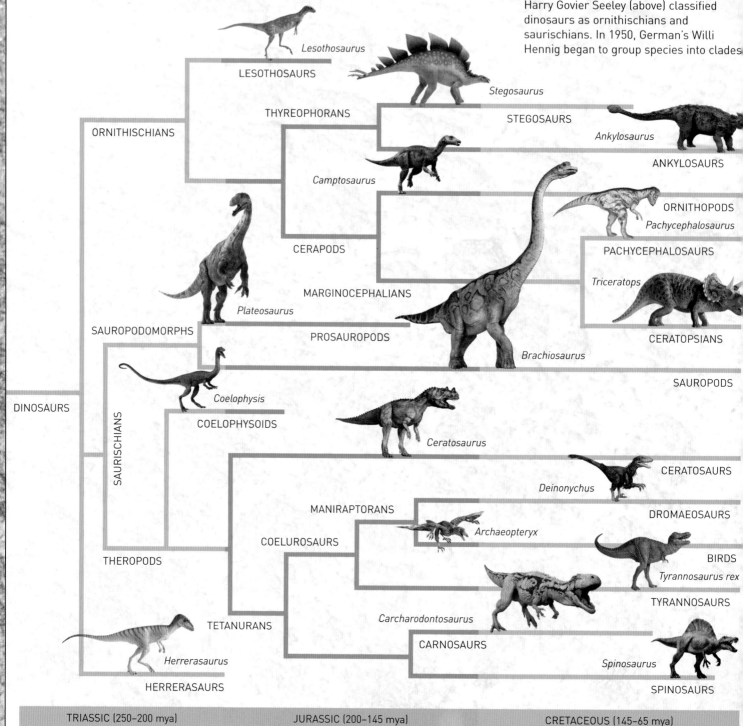

Lesothosaurus

LESOTHOSAURS

Stegosaurus

THYREOPHORANS

STEGOSAURS

ORNITHISCHIANS

Ankylosaurus

ANKYLOSAURS

Camptosaurus

ORNITHOPODS

Pachycephalosaurus

CERAPODS

PACHYCEPHALOSAURS

MARGINOCEPHALIANS

Triceratops

Plateosaurus

SAUROPODOMORPHS

PROSAUROPODS

CERATOPSIANS

Brachiosaurus

SAUROPODS

DINOSAURS

Coelophysis

SAURISCHIANS

COELOPHYSOIDS

Ceratosaurus

CERATOSAURS

Deinonychus

MANIRAPTORANS

DROMAEOSAURS

Archaeopteryx

COELUROSAURS

BIRDS

Tyrannosaurus rex

THEROPODS

TYRANNOSAURS

Carcharodontosaurus

TETANURANS

CARNOSAURS

Herrerasaurus

Spinosaurus

HERRERASAURS

SPINOSAURS

TRIASSIC (250–200 mya)	JURASSIC (200–145 mya)	CRETACEOUS (145–65 mya)

Pronunciation guide

Naming dinosaurs

Most dinosaurs' scientific names are based on Latin or Greek words and each name means something. For instance, *Triceratops* ("three-horned face") describes a special anatomical feature. Many names are tricky to say, but our guide below helps you pronounce many of those in the book.

Name	Pronunciation
Albertosaurus	al BERT oh SORE uss
Allosaurus	allo SORE uss
Alxasaurus	AL shah SORE uss
Amargasaurus	ah MAHR gah SORE uss
Anchisaurus	ankee SORE uss
Ankylosaurus	an KEE loh SORE uss
Apatosaurus	a PAT oh SORE uss
Archaeopteryx	AR kee OP terricks
Argentinosaurus	AR jen TEEN oh SORE uss
Bambiraptor	BAM bee RAP tor
Barapasaurus	buh RAH pah SORE uss
Barosaurus	barrow SORE uss
Barsboldia	bahrs BOHL dee a
Baryonyx	barry ON icks
Brachiosaurus	brackee oh SORE uss
Camarasaurus	KAM a ra SORE uss
Camptosaurus	KAMP toe SORE uss
Carcharodontosaurus	kar KAR oh DON toe SORE uss
Carnotaurus	kar noh TOR uss
Caudipteryx	kor DIP terricks
Centrosaurus	SEN troh SORE uss
Ceratosaurus	seh rat oh SORE uss
Citipati	CHIT i puh tih
Coelophysis	SEE low FYE siss
Compsognathus	KOMP sog NAY thuss
Confuciusornis	CON FYOO shi SOR nis
Corythosaurus	ko RITH oh SORE uss
Cryolophosaurus	KREE o LOAF o SORE uss
Deinocheirus	DIE no KIRE uss
Deinonychus	die NON ee kuss
Dilophosaurus	die LOAF oh sore uss
Diplodocus	di PLOD o kuss
Dryosaurus	DRY oh SORE uss
Edmontonia	ED mon TOE nee a
Edmontosaurus	ed MON toe SORE uss
Eocursor	EE oh KER sor
Eoraptor	EE oh RAP tor
Epidexipteryx	epi dex IP terricks
Euoplocephalus	YOU owe ploh SEFF a luss
Gallimimus	gally MEEM uss
Gastonia	gass TOE nee a
Giganotosaurus	jig anno toe SORE uss
Guanlong	gwahn LOONG
Herrerasaurus	he RAIR a SORE uss
Heterodontosaurus	HET er oh DONT oh SORE uss
Huayangosaurus	HWAH YAHNG oh SORE uss
Hypsilophodon	HIP sill OFF o don
Iguanodon	ig WAHN o don
Kentrosaurus	KEN troh SORE uss

Name	Pronunciation
Lambeosaurus	LAMB ee oh SORE uss
Leaellynasaura	lee EL in a SORE a
Lesothosaurus	le SUE too SORE uss
Maiasaura	MY a SORE a
Majungatholus	mah JOONG gah THOL uss
Mamenchisaurus	ma MEN chee SOREuss
Megalosaurus	MEG ah loh SORE uss
Mei long	may LOONG
Microraptor	MY kro RAP tor
Monolophosaurus	MON o LOAF o SORE uss
Muttaburrasaurus	MUT a BUR a SORE uss
Nigersaurus	nee ZHER SORE uss
Ornithomimus	OR ni thoh MEE mus
Ouranosaurus	OO ran oh SORE uss
Oviraptor	oh vee RAP tor
Pachycephalosaurus	PACK ee SEFF allo SORE uss
Pachyrhinosaurus	PACK ee RYE no SORE uss
Parasaurolophus	PA ra SORE oh LOAF uss
Pentaceratops	PEN ta SERRA tops
Plateosaurus	PLAT ee oh SORE uss
Polacanthus	pol a KAN thuss
Protoceratops	PRO toe SERRA tops
Psittacosaurus	Si tak oh SORE uss
Saltasaurus	SAHL tah SORE uss
Sauropelta	SORE oh PEL ta
Scelidosaurus	SKEL i doe SORE uss
Sinornithosaurus	SIGN or nith o SORE uss
Sinosauropteryx	SIGN o saw ROP terricks
Sinraptor	sign RAP tor
Spinosaurus	SPY no SORE uss
Stegoceras	STEG o SER ass
Stegosaurus	STEG o SORE uss
Styracosaurus	sty RACK oh SORE uss
Tarbosaurus	TAHR bo SORE uss
Tenontosaurus	te NON to SORE uss
Therizinosaurus	THER i ZIN o SORE uss
Triceratops	try SERRA tops
Troodon	TROH o don
Tyrannosaurus	tie RAN o SORE uss
Velociraptor	vell OSS ee RAP tor
Vulcanodon	vul KAN o don

Huayangosaurus

Discovery timeline

Since the first discovery of dinosaur bones in the 1600s, fossil hunters have unearthed and named more than 600 different dinosaurs. Fossils help scientists to work out how dinosaurs moved, fed, fought, bred, and died. This timeline highlights the milestones in the study of dinosaurs.

Roy Chapman Andrews (right)

1677
English curator Robert Plot illustrates part of a *Megalosaurus* thigh bone in a book. He believes it to be the bone of a giant man.

1818
Fossil bones found in Connecticut, USA will later prove to be the first discovery of a North American dinosaur – *Anchisaurus*.

1820
Gideon Mantell, a British doctor, begins to collect fossils of a giant reptile that he later names and describes as *Iguanodon*.

William Buckland

1824
Megalosaurus is the first dinosaur to receive a scientific name when Britain's William Buckland describes its fossil jaw.

1834
American geologist Edward Hitchcock starts collecting dinosaur fossil tracks in Connecticut Valley, USA.

1842
The name "Dinosauria" appears in print for the first time after British anatomist Sir Richard Owen realizes that three kinds of giant fossil reptiles formed part of a special group.

1853
The first lifesize models of dinosaurs are created by Benjamin Waterhouse Hawkins.

1856
American anatomist Joseph Leidy names *Troodon* – the first American dinosaur to be given a scientific name that is still valid.

1859
Dinosaur eggshells are first discovered in the south of France.

1861
German palaeontologist Hermann von Meyer describes *Archaeopteryx*, a bird with feathered wings, but with the teeth and bony tail of a dinosaur.

1877
Huge fossil bones are found in Colorado, USA. By 1890, rival palaeontologists Othniel C Marsh and Edward Drinker Cope discover the fossils of dinosaurs such as *Diplodocus*, *Triceratops*, and *Stegosaurus*.

1878
Belgian coalminers find fossils of dozens of *Iguanodon* at a depth of 322 m (1,056 ft).

1887
British palaeontologist Harry Govier Seeley splits dinosaurs into two main groups – the Saurischia (lizard-hipped) and the Ornithischia (bird-hipped).

1902
American fossil hunter Barnum Brown finds the first *Tyrannosaurus* skeleton in Montana, USA.

1903
American palaeontologist Elmer S Riggs names *Brachiosaurus*, two years after its fossils were found in Colorado, USA.

1908–1912
German palaeontologists Werner Janensch and Edwin Hennig find fossils of late Jurassic dinosaurs, including *Brachiosaurus* and *Kentrosaurus* in Tanzania.

1912–1917
American dinosaur hunter Charles Sternberg and his sons collect a wealth of dinosaur fossils in Alberta, Canada.

1915
German palaeontologist Ernst Stromer von Reichenbach names *Spinosaurus*.

1922–1925
In Mongolia, Roy Chapman Andrews, Henry Fairfield Osborn, and Walter Granger find fossils of dinosaurs including *Oviraptor*, *Protoceratops*, and *Velociraptor*.

1927
In Algeria, French palaeontologists Charles Depéret and J Savornin discover the teeth of *Carcharodontosaurus*.

1933–1970s
Chinese palaeontologist Yang Zhongjian names *Lufengosaurus*, *Mamenchisaurus*, *Tsintaosaurus*, and *Omeisaurus*.

1941
American palaeontologist Roland T Bird describes sauropod footprints, showing that some dinosaurs travelled in herds.

1951
British palaeontologist Kenneth Kermack questions ideas about sauropods, showing that water pressure would have suffocated a snorkelling sauropod.

Carcharodontosaurus skull compared with human skull

1954
Russian palaeontologist Evgeny Maleev discovers the long claws of *Therizinosaurus*.

1965
British palaeontologist Alan Charig works out how dinosaurs evolved from sprawling reptiles.

1969
American palaeontologist John Ostrom argues that dinosaurs' erect limbs meant that they were active and warm-blooded. He also claims that birds evolved from small theropods.

1971
A Polish-Mongolian expedition in Mongolia finds skeletons of a *Velociraptor* and *Protoceratops* locked in battle.

1972
American palaeontologist Robert Bakker suggests that air sacs in some dinosaurs reveal that these must have had a breathing system like that of birds. Later research supports this idea, at least for saurischian (lizard-hipped) dinosaurs.

1974

Palaeontologists Peter Galton and Robert Bakker publish a paper where they argue that birds are actually dinosaurs. Subsequent research provides support for their claim.

Robert Bakker

1978
American palaeontologists John Horner and Robert Makela find the first evidence that dinosaurs cared for their young.

1979
American geologist Walter Alvarez and his nuclear physicist father Luis Alvarez establish that a large asteroid smashed into Earth at the end of the Cretaceous Period with devastating effects.

1980
The first dinosaur fossil – a theropod bone – is found in New Zealand.

1981
Australian Alan Bartholomai and American Ralph Molnar describe the ornithopod *Muttaburrasaurus* from the first nearly complete dinosaur skeleton found in Australia.

1984
British palaeontologist Michael Benton coins the name "Dinosauromorpha" for the group of reptiles consisting of dinosaurs and their closest relatives.

1986
British palaeontologists Alan Charig and Angela Milner describe *Baryonyx*, a fish-eating theropod later identified as a relative of *Spinosaurus*.

1991
American palaeontologist William Hammer excavates *Cryolophosaurus*, the first Antarctic dinosaur to be named.

1993
Argentinian palaeontologists José Bonaparte and Jaimé Powell describe the immense sauropod *Argentinosaurus*.

American palaeontologist Paul Sereno describes *Eoraptor*, the earliest dinosaur to be discovered so far.

1995
Argentinian palaeontologists Rodolfo Coria and Leonardo Salgado describe *Giganotosaurus*, a massive theropod.

1998
Chinese palaeontologists Chen Pei-ji, Dong Zhi-ming, and Zhen Shuo-nan name *Sinosauropteryx*, the first known dinosaur with skin covered in down rather than in reptilian scales.

American palaeontologist Karen Chin describes tyrannosaur fossil dung that contains bones from a horned dinosaur.

2003
Six Chinese palaeontologists describe *Microraptor gui*, a small theropod with feathered arms and legs.

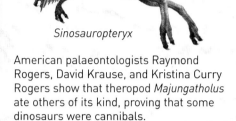
Sinosauropteryx

American palaeontologists Raymond Rogers, David Krause, and Kristina Curry Rogers show that theropod *Majungatholus* ate others of its kind, proving that some dinosaurs were cannibals.

2005
Chinese palaeontologists Meng Jin and Wang Yuanqing find fossils from early Cretaceous China showing that some mammals ate baby dinosaurs.

Swedish scientist Caroline Strömberg shows that some sauropods ate grass in India. Before that, people thought that grass did not exist in the Age of Dinosaurs.

2007
American and Japanese palaeontologists find evidence that some dinosaurs lived in burrows. In an underground den, they found fossils of the ornithopod *Oryctodromeus*.

2008
Belgian palaeontologist Pascal Godefroit and colleagues show that late in the Cretaceous Period, ornithischians and theropods lived and bred in Arctic Siberia.

2009
Mary Schweitzer and colleagues in the USA describe the oldest known protein from an 80-million-year-old hadrosaur's thigh bone. Protein analysis confirms that ornithischian dinosaurs were more closely related to living birds than to alligators.

Palaeontologists at an *Argentinosaurus* dig site

Find out more

There are many ways of finding out about dinosaurs apart from reading books. You can study dinosaur skeletons in museums or see exhibitions of lifelike dinosaur models. You can also take virtual museum tours on the Internet. Then there are dinosaur films and television documentaries that feature scarily realistic models and computer-generated images.

Hunting for dinosaur fossils
Good hunting grounds for fossils include rocks below cliffs that are made of clay, mudstone, and sandstone from the Mesozoic Era. Permission is needed to visit some sites and hunters should keep away from cliffs where rocks could fall.

Museum skeletons
Fossil dinosaurs in museums are made of bones or copies of bones fitted together and supported by rods. The exhibits show how dinosaurs stood when they were alive. Touring exhibitions often include skeletons from distant parts of the world.

Stegosaurus skeleton at the Museum für Naturkunde, Berlin, Germany

Up close
Here, in Pittsburgh's Carnegie Museum of Natural History in the USA, children watch palaeontologist Alan Tabrum tackle the huge and well-preserved skull of Samson, a *Tyrannosaurus rex* – a two-year task.

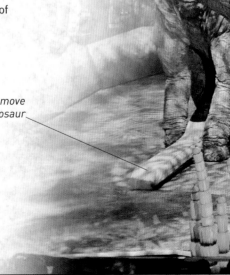

Neck is movable

Sledge to move the dinosaur

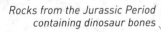

Rocks from the Jurassic Period containing dinosaur bones

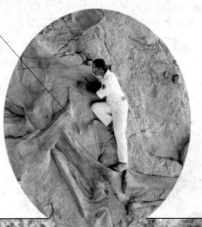

Join a dig!
You might be able to see experts working at a fossil site, or even join in. For years, people have watched palaeontologists carefully ease out bones from rock at the Dinosaur National Monument in Utah, USA.

Real on reel

A *Velociraptor* pack threatens a man in this scene from *Jurassic Park III* (2001). With computer-generated dinosaur images and robotic models, the *Jurassic Park* films were the first to make dinosaurs look lifelike, even though they might not have accurately represented the actual dinosaurs.

Walking with dinosaurs

People can now enjoy live shows with lifelike dinosaurs. The *Walking with Dinosaurs* show tours the world with 15 lifesize models up to 17 m (56 ft) long and 11 m (36 ft) tall.

Audience at the live show

PLACES TO VISIT

NATURAL HISTORY MUSEUM, CROMWELL ROAD, LONDON, UK
- Includes a cast of a *Diplodocus* skeleton and animatronic dinosaurs.

OXFORD UNIVERSITY MUSEUM OF NATURAL HISTORY, OXFORD, UK
- Features the very first *Megalosaurus* bones discovered by William Buckland.

DINOSAUR ISLECULVER PARADE, ISLE OF WIGHT, UK
- Has fossils and animatronic dinosaurs.

MUSEUM FÜR NATURKUNDE INVALIDENSTRASSE, BERLIN, GERMANY
- Includes a *Brachiosaurus*, the world's largest mounted dinosaur skeleton.

AMERICAN MUSEUM OF NATURAL HISTORY CENTRAL PARK WEST, NEW YORK CITY, USA
- Features more than 100 amazing fossil specimens.

FIELD MUSEUM OF NATURAL HISTORY, LAKE SHORE DRIVE, CHICAGO, USA
- Has the world's largest *Tyrannosaurus*.

NATIONAL MUSEUM OF NATURAL HISTORY, WASHINGTON DC, USA
- Holds a huge collection of North American dinosaur fossils.

CARNEGIE MUSEUM OF NATURAL HISTORY, FORBES AVENUE, PITTSBURGH, USA
- Holds a collection of Jurassic dinosaurs.

ROYAL TYRRELL MUSEUM OF PALAEONTOLOGY DRUMHELLER, CANADA
- Displays 40 mounted fossil skeletons.

ZIGONG DINOSAUR MUSEUM DASHANPU, ZIGONG CITY, SICHUAN, CHINA
- Features mid-Jurassic dinosaur fossils.

BEIJING MUSEUM OF NATURAL HISTORY TIANQIAO SOUTH STREET, BEIJING, CHINA
- Displays fossils of feathered dinosaurs.

FUKUI PREFECTURAL DINOSAUR, MUSEUMTERAO, MUROKA, KATSUYAMA, JAPAN
- Has the largest dinosaur display in Japan with 45 skeletons.

Glossary

AMMONITES An extinct group of molluscs related to squid; with a coiled shell. They lived in Mesozoic seas.

AMPHIBIANS A group of cold-blooded vertebrates (backboned animals) that appeared more than 100 million years before the dinosaurs. The young live in fresh water but many grow into land-based adults. Living examples include frogs.

ANKYLOSAURS ("fused lizards") A group of four-legged, armoured, plant-eating ornithischians with bony plates covering the neck, shoulders, and back, and a horny beak used for cropping plants.

Bipedal (*Giganotosaurus*)

ARCHOSAURS A group of extinct and living reptiles with two main subgroups. Crocodiles and their relatives form one group. Dinosaurs, pterosaurs, and their relatives form the other.

ASTEROID A rocky lump orbiting the Sun. Asteroids are smaller than planets but can measure hundreds of kilometres across.

BIPEDAL Walking on two hind limbs, rather than on all fours.

BIRDS A group of dinosaurs with feathered wings. Some scientists call the whole group Aves. Others call the modern birds Aves and refer to the extinct birds as Avialae.

CERATOPSIANS ("horned faces") Plant-eating ornithischians, with a deep beak and a bony frill at the back of the skull. Many, such as *Triceratops*, had facial horns.

COLD-BLOODED Animals that are cold-blooded are dependent upon the Sun's heat for body warmth. Most reptiles are cold-blooded (*see also* WARM-BLOODED).

CONIFER A cone-bearing tree such as a pine or fir.

CRETACEOUS PERIOD Third period of the Mesozoic Era; about 145–65 million years ago.

CYCAD A palm-shaped, seed-bearing plant with long, fernlike leaves. Cycads were common during the Age of Dinosaurs.

DROMAEOSAURIDS ("running lizards") A group of birdlike theropods that were related to birds.

DUCK-BILLED DINOSAURS *See* HADROSAURS

EMBRYO A plant, animal, or other organism in an early stage of development from an egg or a seed.

EVOLUTION The gradual changes in living organisms that occur over many generations. Evolution may result in new species. Dinosaurs gradually evolved from reptile ancestors, and birds evolved, step by step, from dinosaurs.

EXTINCTION The dying-out of a plant or animal species.

FOSSIL The remains of something that once lived, preserved in rock. Teeth and bones are more likely to form fossils than softer body parts, such as skin, muscles, or internal organs.

Cycad

Mammal (*Negabaata*)

GENUS (plural, **GENERA**) In the classification of living organisms, a group of closely related species. The species *Tyrannosaurus rex* belongs to the genus *Tyrannosaurus*.

GINKGO A unique type of broadleaved tree with triangular leaves that evolved in the Triassic Period and survives to this day. A type of gymnosperm.

GYMNOSPERMS One of the two main types of land plants that produce seeds. It includes cycads, ginkgoes, and conifers such as pine and fir.

HADROSAURS ("bulky lizards") Duck-billed dinosaurs. Large, bipedal and quadrupedal ornithopods from late in the Cretaceous Period. They had a ducklike beak that was used for browsing on vegetation.

ICHTHYOSAURS Large prehistoric reptiles with a pointed head, flippers, and a fishlike tail. Ichthyosaurs were streamlined for swimming fast in the sea. Most lived in the Jurassic Period.

JURASSIC PERIOD Second period of the Mesozoic Era; about 200–145 million years ago.

MAMMALS Warm-blooded vertebrates that feed their young on milk. Their skin is covered in hair or fur. Mammals began to appear in the Triassic Period.

MANIRAPTORANS ("grasping hands") A group of theropods with long arms and hands, including dromaeosaurids, such as *Velociraptor*, and birds.

MESOZOIC ("middle life") The geological era, about 250–65 million years ago, containing the Triassic, Jurassic, and Cretaceous periods. From the late Triassic on, dinosaurs were the dominant land animals in the Mesozoic.

MOLLUSCS Snails, clams, squid, and their relatives. Ammonites belonged to a group of molluscs called cephalopods.

MOSASAURS Large, aquatic lizards with paddle-shaped limbs and a flattened tail. They hunted fish and other sea creatures in the Cretaceous Period.

ORNITHISCHIANS ("bird hips") One of the two main dinosaur groups (*see also* SAURISCHIANS). In ornithischians, the pelvis (hip bone) is similar to that of birds. Ornithischians include stegosaurs, ceratopsians, pachycephalosaurs, ankylosaurs, and ornithopods.

ORNITHOPODS ("bird feet") A group of plant-eating ornithischians with long hind limbs. The group includes *Iguanodon* and hadrosaurs.

Palaeozoic Era (Trilobite fossil)

PACHYCEPHALOSAURS ("thick-headed lizards") A group of bipedal ornithischians with a thick skull.

PALAEONTOLOGIST A scientist who studies the fossil remains of plants and animals.

PALAEONTOLOGY The scientific study of fossilized organisms.

PALAEOZOIC ("ancient life") The geological era before the Mesozoic. It lasted from 540 until 250 million years ago.

PLESIOSAURS A group of large marine reptiles living in the Mesozoic Era, often with flipper-shaped limbs and a long neck.

PREDATOR An animal or plant that preys on animals for food.

PROSAUROPODS ("before sauropods") A group of early plant-eating saurischians that lived from late in the Triassic Period to early in the Jurassic Period.

PSITTACOSAURS ("parrot lizards") Bipedal ceratopsians living in the Cretaceous Period. Psittacosaurs had deep beaks like those of parrots and used them to eat plants.

PTEROSAURS ("winged lizards") Flying reptiles of the Mesozoic Era, related to the dinosaurs.

QUADRUPEDAL Walking on all fours.

RADIOACTIVE ELEMENT A substance that decays by giving off particles and energy. Scientists can find the age of fossil-bearing rocks by measuring the radioactivity of elements found in volcanic rocks just above or just below the fossil-bearing rocks.

REPTILES Typically, cold-blooded, scaly vertebrates that lay eggs or give birth on land. Living reptiles include lizards, snakes, turtles, and crocodiles.

SAURISCHIANS ("lizard hips") One of two main dinosaur groups (*see also* ORNITHISCHIANS). In typical saurischians, the hip bones are similar to those of lizards. Saurischians include prosauropods, sauropods, and theropods.

SAUROPODS ("lizard feet") Huge, quadrupedal, plant-eating saurischians, with long necks and tails. They lived through most of the Mesozoic Era.

SCUTE A bony plate with a horny covering to protect the dinosaur from an enemy's teeth and claws.

SEDIMENT Material, such as sand and mud, deposited by wind, water, or ice.

SKULL The bony framework protecting the brain, eyes, ears, and nasal passages.

Fossil droppings

SPECIES The level below genus in the classification of living things. Individuals in a species can breed to produce fertile young. Each species has a two-part name – *Microraptor gui*, for instance.

STEGOSAURS ("plated/roofed lizards") Plant-eating, quadrupedal ornithischians with two tall rows of bony plates running down the neck, back, and tail.

THEROPODS ("beast feet") Mostly predatory saurischians with sharp teeth and claws.

TRACE FOSSIL The remains of signs of prehistoric creatures, rather than fossils of the creatures themselves, preserved in rock. Trace fossils include footprints, bite marks, droppings, eggs, and fossil impressions of skin, hair, and feathers.

TRIASSIC PERIOD First period of the Mesozoic Era; about 250–200 million years ago.

TYRANNOSAURIDS ("tyrant lizards") Huge, bipedal theropods with a large head, short arms, two-fingered hands, and massive hind limbs. Tyrannosaurids flourished late in the Cretaceous Period in North America and Asia.

Sauropod (*Mamenchisaurus*)

VERTEBRATES Animals with a spinal column, or backbone.

WARM-BLOODED Keeping the body at constant temperature (often above that of the surroundings) by turning energy from food into heat. Many dinosaurs were probably warm-blooded, although modern reptiles are not. Mammals and birds are warm-blooded (*see also* COLD-BLOODED).

Index

Acknowledgements

Dorling Kindersley would like to thank:
Sarah Owens for proofreading; Helen Peters for the index; David Ekholm Jalbum, Sunita Gahir, Jo Little, Sue Nicholson, Jessamy Wood, and Bulent Yusuf for the clipart; Sue Nicholson and Jo Little for the wallchart; and Camilla Hallinan for advice.

For this relaunch edition, the publisher would also like to thank: Hazel Beynon for text editing and Carron Brown for proofreading.

The Publishers would like to thank the following for their kind permission to reproduce their photographs:

(Key: a-above; b-below/bottom; c-centre; l-left; r-right; t-top)

Alamy Images: Katewarn Images 18l (Limestone 2), 18l (Limestone); The Natural History Museum, London 61cl, 61tl; vario images GmbH & Co. KG 68cra; Corbis: James L. Amos 57cr; Atlantide Phototravel 62bl; Tom Bean 53tr; Bettmann 21cr, 66tr; Jonathan Blair 2cla, 17r; Gray Braasch 25br (Background); Frank Lane Picture Agency/Derek Hall 68tl; D. Robert & Lorri Franz 28bc; Mark A. Johnson 31bc; Steve Kaufman 18l (Sandstone); Bob Krist 22tl; George D. Lepp 45cr; Louie Psihoyos 28–29c, 46tl, 59br, 60cra, 62tl, 66br, 67cl, 68bc; Louie Psioyos 18tr; Nick Rains 43bl; Roger Ressmeyer 39r; Reuters/Charles Platiau 31cr; Pete Saloutos 35br (Ground

Ferns); Kevin Schafer 12cl, 19tl; Science Faction/Louie Psihoyos 43cla, 45tl; Sygma/Vo Trung Dung 61tr; Zefa/Murat Taner 36cl (Crane); DK Images: Courtesy of The American Museum of Natural History/Lynton Gardiner 6bl, 19tr, 41tr, 59r; Bedrock Studios 57bl; Bedrock Studios/Jon Hughes 17bc, 47l; Robert L. Braun – Modelmaker/Tim Ridley 14br; Courtesy of the Carnegie Museum of Natural History, Pittsburgh/Lynton Gardiner 35cb; Centaur Studios – Modelmaker/Andy Crawford 48bl (Baryonyx); Centaur Studios – Modelmakers/Andy Crawford 23bl; David Donkin – Modelmaker/Andy Crawford 12tl, 14tl; Davin Donkin – Modelmaker/Andy Crawford 10tl; ESPL – Modelmaker/Geoff Brightling 25tc; Graham High – Modelmaker/Gary Ombler 37cra; Graham High at Centaur Studios – Modelmaker/Andy Crawford 36cl (Dinosaur); Graham High at Centaur Studios – Modelmaker/Dave King 23br, 47bc, 49c; John Holmes – Modelmaker/Andy Crawford 33tl; John Holmes – Modelmaker/Steve Gorton 43br; Jon Hughes 15cb (Mososaur), 17br, 24bl, 24br; Jeremy Hunt at Centaur Studios – Modelmaker/Dave King 9tr, 41br; Courtesy of the Museo Argentino De Cirendas Naturales, Buenos Aires 54bl; Courtesy of the Natural History Museum, London 52bl; Courtesy of the Natural History Museum, London/Colin Keates 2tr, 4bl, 4cl, 8c, 20cl, 30tl, 34cb, 34cl, 35ca, 39tr, 41clb, 46bl, 47tr (Diplodocus), 49cl, 51tr, 52–53tc, 55c, 55t, 60–61bl, 62cl, 62–63bc; Courtesy of the Natural History Museum, London/John Downes 2b, 20b, 58br;

Courtesy of the Natural History Museum, London/John Holmes – Modelmaker/John Downes 24clb; Courtesy of the Natural History Museum, London/Philip Dowell 57br; Courtesy of the Naturmuseum Senckenburg, Frankfurt/Andy Crawford 25tl; Courtesy of Oxford University Museum of Natural History/Richard Hammond – Modelmaker/Steve Gorton 24cla; Peabody Museum of Natural History, Yale University. All rights reserved/Lynton Gardiner 49br; Luis Rey 24tl (Panderichthys); Courtesy of the Royal Museum of Scotland, Edinburgh/Harry Taylor 19br; Courtesy of the Royal Tyrell Museum of Paleontology, Alberta, Canada/Andy Crawford 51tc; Courtesy of the Royal Tyrell Museum of Paleontology, Alberta, Canada/Andy Crawford 55bl; Courtesy of the Royal Tyrrell Museum of Paleontology, Alberta, Canada/Andy Crawford 26c, 28bl; Courtesy of the Senckenberg Nature Museum, Frankfurt/Andy Crawford 47tr (Elephant); Courtesy of Staatliches Museum für Naturkunde, Stuttgart/Andy Crawford 1, 32cl; Courtesy of the State Museum of Nature, Stuttgart/Andy Crawford 25tc; Getty Images: AFP/Hector Mata 45c; Brad Barket 69b; The Bridgeman Art Library 21br; Gallo Images/Travel Ink 19cr; Robert Harding World Imagery/Jochen Schlenker 9br (Background); Hulton Archive 21tl; The Image Bank/Doug Allan 24tl (Background); National Geographic/Ira Block 34tl; National Geographic/Jeffrey L. Osborn 8–9c, 29tr, 45tr; Spencer Platt 6cr; Stocktrek Images 17l; Stone/G. Brad Lewis 16tl; Stone/Tim Flach 4tr, 54tl; Stringer/Jeff Swensen 68cb; Taxi/Carl Roessler 15clb (Background); Tetra Images 48bl (Water); Visuals Unlimited/Ken Lucas 64–65 (Background), 66–67 (Background), 68–69 (Background), 70–71 (Background), 71cl; The Kobal Collection: Amblin/Universal/ILM – Industrial Light & Magic 69ca; Columbia Tristar 23tl; Dreamworks/

Paramount 16b; Octávio Mateus: 49tr; The Natural History Museum, London: 20cr, 20tl, 21tr, 26br, 33br, 34bc, 38bl, 50tl, 55cr, 56cl, 56cr, 64tr; Berislav Krzic 29cr; John Sibbick 27br; Photolibrary: Mickey Gibson 18l (Shale 2), 18l (Shale); C.C. Lockwood 18l (Limestone 3); Oxford Scientific/Jen & Des Bartlett 50br; Rex Features: Sipa Press 60tl; Royal Saskatchewan Museum, Canada: 2crb, 33tr; Science Photo Library: Christian Darkin 23ca; Geological Survey of Canada/Mark Pilkington 17cla; Carlos Goldin 67br; Roger Harris 36br; Sheila Terry 66cl; Still Pictures: Biosphoto/Jean-Philippe Delobelle 52cl; Nobumichi Tamura: 57c.

Wallchart: Corbis: Louie Psihoyos (Triceratops), (Palaeontologist); DK Images: Courtesy of The American Museum of Natural History/Lynton Gardiner (Edmontosaurus Mummy); Courtesy of the Natural History Museum, London/John Downes (Nest); Courtesy of Staatliches Museum für Naturkunde, Stuttgart/Andy Crawford (Allosaurus Skull); Getty Images: Gallo Images/Travel Ink (Footprint); National Geographic/Ira Block (Nigersaurus); The Kobal Collection: Dreamworks/Paramount (Deep Impact).

All other images © Dorling Kindersley
For further information see: www.dkimages.com